The Home Stretch

The Home Stretch

Dave Nimmer

NODIN PRESS

ACKNOWLEDGMENTS

I'd like to thank the owners and editors of *Minnesota Good Age Magazine* who paid me a monthly stipend to muse about the vagaries of growing older, and Norton Stillman, owner of Nodin Press, who is a fine example of how to grow old with grace.

9 8 7 6 5 4 3 2 1

ISBN: 978-1-947237-35-3
Library of Congress Control number: 2021937546

Published by
Nodin Press
5114 Cedar Lake Road,
Minneapolis, MN 55416
www.nodinpress.com

Printed in USA

This book is dedicated to all of us who can't believe we're this old: to men who can no longer tie a tiny fly on a gossamer leader, to women who've traded a floral-print bikini for a single-piece swimsuit, and for all of us who try to hide the bottle of Metamucil among the groceries at the checkout counter.

Contents

Foreword

This is not a manual on how to avoid the pitfalls of growing old. It is a collection of experiences that expose the realities of aging, the struggle and heartbreak over losing friends, and the trials presented by an aching body. Balanced against these realities I'd like to place an uptake of humility, the wisdom accrued during decades of being alive, and the virtue of simply surviving.

At first, growing old struck me as a unique experience, but it soon occurred to me how self-centered that perspective was. I suspect it's harder for guys to talk about such things. They keep it to themselves and end up thinking they alone are going through it. That's one reason I wanted to write these stories. But I also wanted to tell them because they helped me to understand where I've been and where I'm headed.

What I do understand is that this part of life—the endgame—is a spiritual journey. The questions are less practical than existential. Why am I here? What am I supposed to do? I have no answers but I have discovered several clues:

– Acknowledge a power greater than yourself. I call it God.

– Admit that you may not be that important anymore, but you're still all you think about all day long. Stop it.

– Give it away: your time, your talent, and a good part of your treasure.

– Recognize, as simple as it sounds, that love is the only thing that matters.

– Listen to more music.

– Do it all one day at a time.

Will this prescription help you grow old gracefully? Not necessarily, but it will make you less of a pain in the ass—both to yourself and to those around you.

A Very Good Friday

I wasn't planning to go to church that night—it was Good Friday—since it was cold, grey, and damp, and I was looking forward to the TV broadcast of a NBA game. But I got a call from Pastor John Matthews asking me to read a little scripture for the service, and I wasn't in the habit of saying No to him.

When I got to Memorial Lutheran Church of Afton, on the hillside overlooking the St. Croix River, it was quiet inside, with shafts of soft, grey light coming through the windows. A cross was tipped on its side and draped in a black cloth in front of the sanctuary. It was a somber setting, perfect for the event we were about to recall and remember.

I sat in a chair next to the pastor, to the right of the pulpit, and watched the parishioners trudge in, silently and reverently. The choir was already seated and the organist was softly playing what sounded like a funeral dirge. It was impossible to miss the mood and message of the service to come.

I began my reading from scripture with Matthew, Chapter 27, verses 21 through 25:

> *Which of the two do you want me to release to you? asked the governor. "Barabbas," they answered. "What shall I do, then, with Jesus who is called the Messiah?" Pilate asked. They all answered, "Crucify him." "Why? What crime has he committed?" asked Pilate. But they shouted all the*

louder, "Crucify hm." When Pilate saw that he was getting nowhere, but that instead an uproar was starting, he took water and washed his hands in front of the crowd. "I am innocent of this man's blood," he said. "It is your responsibility." All the people answered, "His blood is on us and on our children."

On this night, the words of condemnation from the crowd in front of Pilate seemed so callous and cruel. For one of the few times in my checkered life as a Christian, I was able to see in flesh and form the words I was reading. My voice cracked and I struggled to finish the last verse.

In truth, I had not spent a lot of time reading scripture, singing hymns, or attending church between my high school graduation and my middle-age moderation. During those years I was earnestly trying a program of self-will, self-restraint, and self-control—with varying degrees of success. When I left the church as an eighteen-year-old, Protestants I knew were worried that nuns would take over public schools if John Kennedy was elected president. That was enough for me to take my leave.

By the time I came back for another look at the Christian faith, 35 years later, I had been down on my knees several times, sucking for air and asking for mercy. My record of running my own affairs left a lot to be desired. And I had lied to my father when he asked whether I was going to church. Sure, Dad, I'm going to church. What I didn't say was that it happened twice a year, at Christmas and Easter.

After he died, I had this nagging feeling it was time to set things straight. I joined Memorial, and here I was on a somber Good Friday, reading from the Gospel of Matthew:

12

*Then the governor's soldiers took Jesus into the Praetorium
and gathered the whole company of soldiers around him.
They stripped him and put a scarlet robe on him and then
twisted a crown of thorns and set it on his head. They put a
staff in his right hand. Then they knelt in front of him and
mocked him. "Hail, king of the Jews," they said.*

After I finished this verse, the congregation got its chance
to get in the mood themselves, and they did, with a spirited
rendition of "Were You There When They Crucified My
Lord?" I have always loved that melody and, somehow, my
limited range is suited to the chorus: "Ooh, ooh, ooh, ooh,
sometimes it causes me to tremble, tremble, tremble. Were
you there when they crucified my Lord?"

This song was likely composed by African-American slaves
in the 19th century, and it helps to remind me that Our Lord
Jesus probably had a little color in his blood, too, though you'd
never guess it on the basis of the Presbyterian and Lutheran
upbringing I received. On that Friday night, the white people
at Memorial sang with soul. I was proud of them.

As a matter of fact, I felt more connected to the people in
the church that night than I ever had before. It was as though
we had all arrived in the same frame of mind and were looking
for the same experience when we got there. We were appro-
priately reserved and respectful. We were quiet. We wanted to
connect with the events we were reading about in the gospels.
The last one I read was from John, Chapter 19:

*Later, knowing that everything had now been finished,
and so that Scripture would be fulfilled, Jesus said, "I am
thirsty." A jar of wine vinegar was there, so they soaked a
sponge in it, put the sponge on a stalk of the hyssop plant,*

and lifted it to Jesus' lips. When he had received the drink,
Jesus said, "It is finished." With that, he bowed his head
and gave up his spirit.

I was glad to be finished. I wasn't sure I could get through much more without straining and stumbling over the words. This was the most emotional experience I'd ever had in church, and I had no clue as to why, but I was going to ride it all the way to the finish.

As the service came to an end, Pastor Matthews invited the parishioners to come up to the altar as they left, to kneel in front of the cross, say their prayers, and then leave quietly into the evening. I had a front row seat for the procession. Matthews was kneeling at one end of the cross and I noticed a hole in the sole of one of his shoes. Somehow it seemed to fit the notion of humility that pervaded the church.

Parishioners came up two by two, four by four, one by one. They were young and old, healthy and compromised, connected and alone. The first I noticed were an elderly couple I knew, both retired school teachers who were about to give up their townhome for an assisted-living apartment.

Al and Arlene walked down the aisle slowly, deliberately, Arlene with her hand on Al's elbow, gently guiding him along. It took them at least a minute to get on their knees. And they needed the pastor to help them to their feet again. They were still bent over as they left the sanctuary, hand in hand.

Not soon after them came a family of four; the kids were pre-teens and the parents in their late thirties. They were dressed well and, compared to Al and Arlene, they were sprightly. What I was struck with, though, was how quiet, reverent, and respectful the kids were. They seemed to understand the gravity of the moment, of the evening.

Toward the end of the procession a single man approached the altar. He was middle aged, with a scruffy, grey beard and hair to match. I had heard that he'd gone through a tough divorce from which he'd never quite recovered. I recall that he later made the coffee for the social hour that followed the church services. On this night, I felt I ought to put my arm around his shoulders as he knelt at the cross. He, too, got up and walked away.

By now the choir was singing the chorus: "Jesus, Remember Me, When You Come into Your Kingdom." It sounded both plaintive and poignant. Tears ran down my cheeks for one of the few times in my life. I've rarely been able to cry, even when I lost loved ones. On this night I did.

Part of it was the music, but beyond that and more important was the feeling of gratitude: I was completely at peace, overwhelmed by the notion that I was exactly where I ought to be, doing exactly what I ought to do and that all would be well with my soul. I'd never before felt anything like that.

Before I left the church, I knelt beside John Matthews in front of the cross. My prayer was simply Thank You. I got up and walked out into the evening. A light mist was falling. I got in the car and sang the refrain "Jesus, Remember Me" all the way home.

On Easter Sunday, I went back to the church on a sunny, warm morning. I walked in, sat in the middle pew and looked around. The feeling was gone.

A Key(board) to My Past

One of the first sounds I can remember is my mother playing the piano. I grew up in a home with a Steinway baby grand in the living room and a mother who could play it very well. She was naturally skilled and classically trained.

She graduated from the Wisconsin College of Music in Milwaukee, the music conservatory at Lawrence College in Appleton, Wisconsin, and the Chicago College of Music. "As a child artist," her obituary stated, "she was acclaimed a child prodigy by her instructors, music critics and audiences. She appeared at the Garrick Theater and was billed as 'the 8-year-old child wonder.'"

The child wonder never did pursue a professional career, but she gave piano lessons, served on a symphony board, and played the organ at the First Presbyterian Church in Fond du Lac, Wisconsin. She died much too young at the age of forty-nine, and I never did tell her how good she was and how much I learned to love the classical music that informed her life.

She and her mother, Grandma Edith, tried their best to teach me piano. I believe they both secretly hoped I had gotten the music gene, but after seven years of lessons from Edith, it was apparent to them both—and to me—that I had not.

Oh, in seven years, I learned how to play scales, to read music (haltingly) and even to memorize some of it. My most ambitious attempt was playing Edvard Grieg's Peer Gynt Suite with its easily recognized final movement, "In the Hall of the Mountain King." Critics have said that the movement is impossible to dislike or forget. They obviously didn't hear my recital as a twelve-year-old. I forgot a portion, I misplayed a portion, and I labored through the rest.

The review from Grandma Edith was that I was earnest, loud, and brave. She knew how frightened I was and she saw me sweat. Grieg would bring to an end my piano career. Mother and Grandma agreed that writing and public speaking might be a better fit for my talents. I didn't mind, and I started spending my summer Saturday mornings playing softball and fishing.

As I got older, I kind of wished I had kept up with the lessons so that at least I could play some simple melodies. The feeling came back stronger in my mid-seventies when I began attending monthly Taize Prayer sessions at the Basilica of St. Mary that involved singing repetitive, uncomplicated songs.

The melodies are lovely and lingering, and I got to think-ing: Maybe I could learn to pick these out on a keyboard and sit in my den and hold my own "service." I mentioned this to a friend and one day awoke to find a box from Amazon on my doorstep with the morning paper. He'd been planning to buy a keyboard for his son's birthday and decided to make it two.

At first I tried to follow the instructions on how to play the thing, using the small screen on the keyboard that shows you where to put your fingers for any of the ninety songs in the Casio instructional book, but I found that I couldn't fol-low along; the images were too small and moved too quickly. So I decided to learn, again, how to read music, starting with the treble clef. O.K. That's middle "C" and then, and then, it's D, E ,F, G, A, B and back to C. It took me about a week to get that straight and transfer it to my right hand.

I hit some clinkers, especially when the piece had sharps or flats. That's a little road sign I invariably missed at first, and the oversight would send that pretty little melody into the ditch. But I got better, noting that F sharp and C sharp were the most common and that old B flat hung right behind.

So I got the right hand moving with alacrity and assurance, but I still had the left hand to worry and wonder about. I mean, what looks like a B flat on the treble clef is a D on the bass clef. C on the treble is E on the bass, and on it goes. I have managed to put both those clefs, and the hands that play them, together on a couple of simple pieces: "Ubi Caritas" and "Calm Me, Lord."

I'm spending about 45 minutes to an hour a couple times a week at this keyboard: starting, stopping, looking, searching and stretching. I haven't forgotten how far it is for my fingers between an octave; it's just that at seventy-eight, my fingers don't stretch that easily anymore. Sometimes I have to smile as I struggle.

But I'm learning something. I'm using my mind. I'm stimulating the synaptic connections somewhere in the back of my brain. A doctor friend of mine tells me there's evidence such stimulation wards off early onset dementia. More than that, it's nice to believe I can still learn something.

While I'm practicing I am not watching television. Of course, I'm missing such enlightening features as *Pawn Stars, The Bachelor, Keeping Up With the Kardashians*, and *Pit Bulls and Parolees*. Most important of all, I am making music. However simple the melody, it's still music. And I am the guy with the fingers on the keys.

I am, however, under no illusions. One night I thought I was playing particularly well and I called the friend who had given me the keyboard. "Listen to this rendition of 'Amazing Grace'," I said. Then I put the phone next to the keyboard and placed my hands on the keys.

I got through the first bar. Then I hit a wrong key. Next I messed up a bass-clef chord. Then my finger slipped and I hit two keys at once. By the time I finished, I was sweating— sweating over an audience of one at the other end of the phone line. "Let me play that again," I said.

"No," he replied, "I got the idea."

So did I. The date for my first recital has yet to be determined. But my friend's experience has given me a ray of hope. He took up the piano upon his retirement, hiring a teacher and buying a baby grand. He took weekly lessons, practiced regularly, and told me he was making real progress. After a year and a half, he took part in a Sunday recital for his teacher's pupils.

I attended. Some of the students were quite accomplished, and a few were going on to music schools. My buddy looked accomplished walking up to the stage, dressed in black slacks and a black turtle neck, carrying the score to Pachelbel's Canon in D. He put his hands on the keys, stared at the music, and began to play.

Somewhere between the first measure and the last chord, he and Pachelbel got separated and eventually lost each other. When it was over, he raised his head, grabbed the music, and carefully, carefully, stepped down from the stage.

At the reception afterword, I thought I offered a most appropriate comment, gentle but honest. "Pal," I said, "you showed great courage today. I'm proud of you. And I'm glad your kids weren't around to hear it."

Two years later he played again, at his home, on the occasion of his fiftieth wedding anniversary. It was classical, clean and quite lovely. He got an ovation. And I had a thought: If one old dog can learn to sit up, well ...

The Commencement Speech

In my experience, the commencement speech is usually predictable, forgettable and, in a few instances, even regrettable. I've given a few myself. Not long ago, as I was sorting through some old records and papers from my teaching days at The University of St. Thomas, I came across a mid-year commencement speech I gave to a couple of hundred seniors.

It was a year after 9/11, and when I reread it, I'll admit I liked what I had to say—probably because I was talking to myself:

> *Congratulations upon your graduation from The University of St. Thomas. I am grateful to speak to you today because I came here from the world of work and commerce I suspect many of you are anxious to enter.*
>
> *I spent twenty-six years as a reporter and editor, collecting weekly paychecks, passing around a business card with my name on it, climbing upward on the newsroom table of organization and trying to win one of those journalistic prizes to set me apart from the rest of the pack. And I suspect I thought I had placed my college days behind me, that I'd never have to read a book again I'd have to remember. I wouldn't have to struggle through a poem whose meaning eluded me and I wouldn't be expected to stick my hand in the air and answer a question about the required*

reading. At least not at 8:30 on a Monday morning.

Well, at the age of 49, I came back to campus – this one – to teach journalism. In 11 years here, I've been blessed with an occasional insight, enabling me to reorder priorities in my life. Relax. I'm not going to preach at you. But I'd like to prod you a bit by sharing a few of my struggles and a couple lessons relearned.

They begin with a realization of the interdependence of the parts and people of this world. One discipline is linked to another. New theories in physics instruct new possibilities for theology. Aristotle's Golden Mean is as relevant in a journalism ethics class or a broadcast newsroom as it is at a philosophy round table.

One person is dependent upon another, a neighborhood upon a city, a state upon a country, one nation upon another. Our own self-interest is inextricably linked with that of the human condition. The point was graphically and tragically made for me with the attack on America [The World Trade Towers]. I believe the U.S. was poised to isolate itself from the policies and problems of the rest of the world. Now our battle against terrorism will succeed to the degree a world community is mobilized and stays together.

The same can be said for life within America's boundaries. Our society doesn't become what it could be unless we take all of our citizens along for the ride. That means the single mother who's seeking an affordable place to live, the youngster who's looking for someone to care whether he's in school or not, or a recent immigrant who's seeking a job... or maybe just directions on which bus to take.

I ran into dozens of these people as a reporter. I got my story, said goodbye and wished them well. And I went about my business. Here at St. Thomas, I ran into a *sociology professor who made it his business to be involved in their business: those who were stuck in the quagmire of poverty.*

We were telling their story in a documentary. But after the shooting was done, my sociology colleague was not. He took a kid to the doctor. He cleaned out a house. He found a tutor for a struggling junior high student. He paid a past-due phone bill. Most of all, he cared in a deeper way than I ever had about the subjects of the stories he was telling.

In some ways, that was a revelation. The richness, the significance, the essence of reporting and storytelling were about others, not about the reporter. It was not about me. It was about them and their lives.

I'll bet you've run into a fellow student at St. Thomas who's taught you a lesson about doing for others. On this day, I think of a former student who's spending time with her mother as her Mom battles cancer. This young woman has taught me something about courage, commitment and compassion.

For a long time I had trouble getting in touch with the feeling side of me — those emotions that I could never quite drag to the surface. These days it's easier, in part because I was able to renew a long-standing love of music. When you're chasing stories and meeting deadlines, music doesn't seem to matter as much.

But some afternoons at St. Thomas I would slip over to the chapel, sit quietly in a back pew, take off my shoes, put up my feet and listen to Andrew Hackett, a student, play the organ. Sometimes he rumbled and roared. Sometimes he whispered and worshipped. Wherever the chords led, I followed. And I followed the blues riffs of Chris Kachian (a professor of music) on the mouth harp, as he accompanied the liturgical choir as it practiced a soulful spiritual of toil and trouble.

For me music is pure feelings: goose bumps, chills and sometimes tears streaming down your face. It's what I like about church when it gets good. It's what stays with me in the aftermath of terrorism: the first time I heard a New York City patrolman on the mound at Yankee Stadium singing God Bless America or a mezzo soprano from the Metropolitan Opera with all verses of Amazing Grace.

If St. Thomas helped me to listen again, it also taught me to read again. Someone over lunch in The Grill might ask you whether you've read the required freshman text, Heaven's Coast, or seen David McCullough's biography of Harry Truman.

The Dean of the College, upon hearing of your long-planned trip to Alaska, might lend you his copy of John McPhee's book, Coming into the Country, *and you'd read:*

"Alaska runs off the edge of the imagination, with its tracklessness, its millions of acres of wilderness, its beyond-the-ridgeline surprises."

And then you'd run into a student who'd tell you about a class she was taking from Leslie Adrienne Miler (professor of English). And you'd go to the book stores and find a small volume of her poetry, I was caught by a poem entitled "Temporary Services."

> *"Each morning now I go to the calculator*
> *And take a moment to run my rate of pay*
> *Against the hours, remind myself what*
> *I'm worth to them. To this world which is,*

> After all substantial. And I am trying to find
> A way to take heart in with me, but I see
> How the best lines wither under the repetition
> Or the functional: "Information services –
> Help you. Two days to find out what
> They produce here. Reams of numbers, words
> Cold and dry as paper in the mouth."

All I can say is "Wow." When words are stitched together with crispness and clarity, with gravity or grace, style and spirit, the message has an impact. Whether you're writing to a woman you love or a man you'd just as soon get rid of, why not do it with style and grace? Sharing your prose, your writing, is an act of generosity. And I have discovered at St. Thomas that nothing in my life is truly worthwhile unless I give some of it away.

That goes for my money, my time and my talent, whatever it is. The dictionary definition is mentoring. The real-life meaning is sharing what you have. The most dynamic act of this sharing I've discovered is teaching. What it required from me was cognizance, compassion, courage and candor – the honesty to admit when I was wrong or did not know. What it required from students was persistence, patience and passion.

And when we had it cooking, when the MOJO was working, the semester flew by – a hearty stew of ideas, stories and techniques.

For me, the reward was symbolized in a postcard from San Francisco from two young women in a broadcast reporting class. They were travelling across the country in the first two weeks of June, visiting television newsrooms trying to find the right job. They wrote:

"Nim. We saw the sea lions for you on Pier 39. All is going very well. Even if we don't get a job, this trip has been worth it. We've made some good connections. Hell, we can always write a book on how to plan a road trip. We'll see you when we get back. And don't worry, Nim. We'll remember you when we're famous."

The card is signed Angela and Chantel.

I can't think of a better reason to be a mentor. And I can't think of a better lesson to take away from this place for me – and you. The fact is St. Thomas is rich in ideas, skills and theories. arts and sciences, the practical and the sublime. If you're like me, you'll want to take some of this along on your journey.

I wish you a sweet walk in the life ahead, filled with good music, graceful prose and generous spirits.

I suppose if I'd been in the audience instead of at the podium, I might have been dozing by now. It dawned on me—at this stage of my life—that perhaps I ought to be paying attention. The truth is I was talking to myself.

"Pop" and the Prodigal Son

Willie Wallace calls me "Pops" and I'm old enough to be his father, maybe even his grandfather.

I met him in the mid 90s when I took my journalism reporting class at the University of St. Thomas over to The City, an alternative school and youth center on East Lake Street in Minneapolis. The clients were those who got kicked out of public schools, got into trouble with the law, or suffered in dysfunctional families.

The City was kind of a last resort before a kid ended up in jail or on the streets. Minneapolis cops thought it was a refuge for guns and drugs, but supporters, including rich, white businessmen, talked about the lives that were saved. Will Wallace was clearly among those in the lifeboat.

A native of Clarksdale, Mississippi, Willie came to Minneapolis with his mother as a youngster. He was a promising baseball player, with a wicked fast ball. But it wasn't long before he fell in with a different crowd that promised easy money and a formidable reputation. He joined the Gangster Disciples and soon had his own street name: Chill Will.

He and his group of "home boys" were in the fast lane of the street life: selling drugs, marking territory, making money and always, always looking over their shoulders. Then one day Will got caught up in a street robbery, got busted, and received a break from the judge. With help from a counselor at The City, he turned to a different path. He got his G.E.D. and took a job at The City.

When I and my class met him on that spring morning, he was running the daycare center and, to his surprise, he turned out to be good at it. He was also good at describing the inner-city street life to eighteen of my mainly suburban, all-white college juniors. He got their attention when he opened his mouth.

"I was good at what I did," he said, "and on the mean streets they knew better than to mess with Chill Will. I was runnin' wild and slingin' drugs, with a book of steady custom-ers and a pocket full of $100s."

Then he quietly talked of the tough times, growing up without a father, worrying about who could pay the rent and buy the groceries, losing his connection with baseball, the game that spawned dreams of fame and fortune.

He told my Tommie students they were lucky to be in college, learning a craft, preparing for a job. He was trying to support a couple of kids, pay his rent and get a promotion to a job that paid more than $20,000 a year. But he assured them he wasn't giving up and had his sights on something bigger and better.

He told that story to a couple of classes of students I brought to The City. Then one morning I walked into my classroom on the St. Thomas campus and Will Wallace was in the back of the room, hands folded on the table and a smile on his face. He'd come to check out the campus and the students he'd been talking to, thinking maybe he had a chance.

After class we talked and then I spoke with Tom Helge-son, a friend of mine who did public relations work for The City. Tom had talked Will into checking out the classroom and I expressed my doubts to Helgeson. "Will has only got a

G.E.D.," I said, "and he can't write very well. And he doesn't have any computer skills. We'd just be setting him up to fail."

"Let him decide that," Helgeson said, and together we made our pitch to the Dean of Students to accept Will.

She said he'd have to take a summer remedial course, Bridge for Success, and if he successfully completed that, he'd be provisionally accepted to St. Thomas. Will spent three summer months studying, writing, reading, and taking tests. He walked over the bridge and started in the fall of 1998 as a freshman at The University of St. Thomas.

That St. Thomas had a reputation as a haven for rich, white suburban kids (largely untrue) didn't seem to faze Will. He jumped into the scene, taking three courses, keeping his job at The City, and even participating in extra-curricular campus life.

I recall seeing him on closed-circuit television as a co-host of CampusScope, a student-produced program. Will was on set, sitting in an overstuffed chair, giving his take on campus life; he wasn't shy about sharing his street perspective. The next fall he picked up a camera and shot some of the football action for the Tommies' sports department.

He clearly aimed to be part of university life, and a couple of his sociology professors told me they appreciated his willingness to share thoughts and feelings with students in the class. Sociology was his favorite subject, probably because he lived so much of what he was reading about.

He once told me that he learned about his own racial history, particularly the underground slave railroad and the migration of southern blacks to the big cities of the north from the 1940s through the 1970's. "I got to go to a white man's college," he said, smiling "to learn about a black man's history."

Will Wallace and me at a fundraiser

The most poignant moments of Will's college career were his last, two years after he started. I got a call one spring morning from Will, asking me to meet him in the quad in front of the library. I brought his faculty friend and mentor Steven Lybrand, a sociology professor who took a personal interest in Will.

We found Will sitting on a bench with a letter in his hands and tears in his eyes. The letter from the dean informed him he was on probation, no longer eligible to take classes. His grade point was too low, a victim of courses in beginning German and Old Testament theology. " That's it," he said, "I'm done." He seemed profoundly sad and disappointed.

We told him he could come back, but we both knew that'd be unlikely. He had already racked up thousands of dollars of student loans that still cause me to be angry at the financial aid office. I should have been more watchful. Also, Will already had too little time, with a job and a family. And the courses were now getting more intense and demanding. That morning was his last on campus as a student.

But he did parlay those two years of college into several jobs with non-profits working with at-risk youth. He really found his niche with Emerge, and its North Four program in north Minneapolis. The program provides training, employment and counseling for young men, many of whom were in gangs and most of whom came from dysfunctional families. Officially, Will is the director.

Unofficially, Will is the program's on-call mentor, part-time father and sometimes spiritual confessor. One day he'll have to find a place for a kid to sleep. The next he'll have to replace the money for tennis shoes and jeans that was stolen by a boy's drug-addicted mother.

Will cares about his guys because, once, he was a street guy. He knows how to find the young brothers. He knows how to listen. He knows what to say: Keep doing what you're doing – drugging and dealing – and your worlds will be small. Your troubles will grow. Your peace will be gone. More than likely, your life will be short.

The alternative, he admits, isn't easy. Come in (from the streets). Get trained. Go to work. Stay at it. And think about going back to school. During one stretch, Will reached out to 113 young men. All of them stayed alive, half of them got jobs, and seven went to college. Those are some of the most impressive numbers I've seen in my life—coming against all odds.

Will brought some of his Emerge kids over to St. Thomas while I was still teaching. One early summer night we walked out to the football field, with its green turf, purple seats, and giant scoreboard. Some of the kids had never been across the Mississippi River from Lake Street to Marshall Avenue.

Will made the point: "I told you guys," he said, "don't let your world be small, from Plymouth to Broadway, Lyndale to Penn." He told them to dream a little bigger, work a little harder, be a little bolder. I don't know about the young brothers, but I was ready to saddle up and ride.

Will got a little bolder as he got older, and he took up my invitation to meet the north side nuns, seven Sisters of the Visitation living in two houses on Fremont and Girard Avenues. I told him he and the sisters had the same goal of bringing peace and promise to the neighborhood.

Will took Sister Mary Frances Reis up on an invitation to bring a couple of boys he was working with to a Catholic youth camp on Big Sandy Lake, near McGregor, Minnesota. The nuns had been sponsoring neighborhood children to the camp for years. They prodded the parents, paid the tab, arranged the transportation, and handled the logistics. Will went along one day for the ride.

He quickly discovered that Mary Frances and the other sisters were the real deal: street savvy, worldly wise, yet sincerely spiritual. It's a combination that drew him in and kept him going. Over the years, the Vis sisters occasionally helped him pay the rent, buy some groceries, and comfort his soul. When his brother was shot and killed in Mississippi, Will drove to the Girard house on Christmas morning for comfort and consolation.

He's returned the favors whenever he can. He and his Emerge brothers have delivered the nuns' holiday packages, moved their furniture, and shoveled their sidewalks. And when the sisters asked, Will showed up to talk with neighbors, supporters and students. When he tells his story, the room gets quiet.

Will, Mary Frances, and I have shared a few quiet

dinners at Broadway Pizza. We talk of troubles and triumphs, and Will and I usually start eating before Mary Frances interrupts: "Gentlemen, a prayer before we eat, please. And let's not forget the gratitude."

Will and I are most grateful when we're in my fourteen-foot AlumaCraft fishing boat on a lake in Afton. I discovered Will liked to fish in 2001. He told me he was getting up early on Saturday mornings and heading out to Lake Minnetonka. He found a spot on the bank of Brown's Bay and cast a bobber and night crawler for bass.

Will learned to fish on a small, cold-water creek in Mississippi, catching catfish with a cane pole. The passion stayed with him, even through his drugging and dealing days. It brought him peace when nothing else would.

So I invited Will to go fishing one late summer afternoon. I was a bit uneasy because my boat is small and Will is big—250 pounds give or take a few. I need not have worried. He knew how to get in, sit down and set up to fish. He was using my spinning rod, with a plastic worm and a splitshot about a foot above it. It's a tough rig to fish properly if you're not used to it. Will got acquainted in five minutes.

I had to smile. He was born to fish, totally involved and perfectly comfortable. Over the years, Will and I have caught several hundred bass, a few northerns, and a couple of meals of crappies.

I believe we're pretty even and, when we're together, the fish usually bite—even at midday in midsummer. Will's got a faster retrieve than I do and usually catches the first fish. I come on slower and stronger and we are well aware of each other's tendencies and eccentricities.

After the second trip with Will, I discovered he's a fish whisperer. He talks to them. "C'mon, big girl," he'll say, usually with a smile. "I know you're there. And I'm gonna let you go. I just want your company for awhile."

Toward the end of one of our fishing trips, Will looked at me from his seat in the bow. "Pops," he said, "someday I'd like to have you in *my* boat, on a little lake down in Mississippi. We'd fish bass in the morning and maybe go to a secret river I know about and catch catfish in the afternoon. In the evening we'd go get some barbecue and then I'd take you to a backwoods, roadhouse bar where you'd be the only white man in the place. And we'd listen to some blues."

One more reason to hang around.

You've Got Cancer

I think I was eleven years old when I first heard the word cancer. I'd just returned from a week's vacation with my grandmother and grandfather at Lake Winnebago in Wisconsin. Grandpa Henry and I had rowed a boat into a slough, hunted for turtles and looked for frogs. I loved the idea that he was always up for poking around and chasing critters. My Dad was too practical, asking me what I'd do with one when I caught it. Grandpa Henry never asked, but when I did catch a couple of frogs, he always managed to persuade me somehow to let 'em go. That day, while we were in the boat, he told me he was going to the doctor when he got back to Fond du Lac, that he'd been having some trouble peeing. That's all he said.

My mother told me later that after his doctor visit and a follow-up hospital exam, Grandpa had been diagnosed with prostate cancer. She said it had travelled to his bones and his condition was serious. Over the next few months, I watched him lose weight, lose control (of his bladder) and lose interest in things. He stayed home, and I was always uneasy when I'd see this big wet spot on the front of his pants. I was old enough to feel bad for this man who always had his hair combed, his pants pressed, and his shoes polished.

Grandpa Henry rarely got out of bed the month before he died, and it scared me to see him in such obvious pain. After he died, my grandmother took the three of us—Mom, Dad, and me—on a train trip to California. Fewer than five months after we got back, *she* died of liver cancer. My mother was her chief caregiver.

Five years later my mother would die, at the age of forty-nine, from ovarian cancer. I was twenty-one, a senior at the University of Wisconsin. The summer I spent with my mother at our home in Fond du Lac scared the daylights out of me. The chemotherapy she'd received at the University hospital had almost killed her. By the end of the summer, she weighed less than eighty pounds. Her teeth were too big for her face. Her arms were black and blue. And this woman who used to play "Claire de Lune" effortlessly on the Steinway baby grand in our living room could not feed herself.

All of the prayers for healing were in vain; nothing seemed to ease her pain. I can remember the nurses in the hospital refusing to give her a morphine shot because "it wasn't time." Mom would cry out in pain. I should have walked up to the nursing station and DEMANDED relief for her. I didn't. I just stayed with her as long as I could stand it and then I left, feeling guilty.

Mom died just before I started my last semester in college. I came away from Madison with a bachelor's degree in journalism and a fatalistic fear of cancer. It subsided over the years, especially when I was out gathering stories, getting married, making friends, and taking trips. The decades of my thirties, forties, and fifties were marked by poor habits but good health. I had my tonsils out, suffered with sinus congestion and an occasional prostate infection.

As I approached sixty, my PSA numbers started to rise. I had a prostate biopsy that found no cancer. A year later, I had another biopsy. Soon after, I got a telephone message to call a doctor at Metro Urology. I knew what it was. I knew what he'd say. What I didn't know was how I'd behave or what I'd do.

When I got the word that, indeed, I had prostate cancer, I went out to mow the lawn—three acres of grass—with a walk-behind mower where I could push, pull, and sweat. My friend and companion, Cindy Lamont, was standing on the patio deck watching me. She ran up and hugged me, saying she didn't want me to die.

"I'm not going to die," I said. Caught in time, prostate cancer is survivable, and the surgery to remove the prostate is as mundane as the tonsillectomy of 50 years ago. With Cindy at my side, I talked with the urologist and decided on a date for surgery to be done using the da Vinci System, "a robotic technology that allows the surgeon's hand movements to be translated into smaller, precise movements of tiny instruments inside the patient's body."

That's what the website said. The surgeon I chose had done hundreds of these procedures and when I asked, he nodded that, yes, he WAS good at video games. By the time I arrived at St. John's Hospital for surgery, Cindy and I had sat through an informational session with forty other guys and their partners about impotence and incontinence. They served finger sandwiches and bottled water. I dared Cindy to think of a more memorable "date."

The surgery went well. Doctors removed the cancerous prostate. Surrounding lymph nodes were clear. My recovery was quick and uneventful. The only concern, my surgeon told me, was that some of the cancerous tissue was near the edge of the prostate, increasing the likelihood that some cells remained in my belly. For three years, none appeared. Then, my PSA went from undetectable to detectable. What the PSA count was likely detecting were cancer cells, according to the doctors I consulted.

I decided to get radiation treatments to kill those that

remained. The radiation was five days a week, about ten to fifteen minutes a day, for eight weeks. The process was painless, almost comfortable, except for the full bladder I was to have during each session. That apparently minimized damage to surrounding organs.

The staff at Minnesota Oncology was young, responsive, and personable. I realized again what I learned following the surgery: the real heroes of medicine are the nurses, technicians, orderlies, and aides who empty your bags, dress your wounds, take your vitals, position your body, adjust the beam, and push the button.

I learned something about the kindness of strangers. It is, of course, their job to minister to you according to their specialty. But some of them do it with such generosity and grace, such humor and humanity, insight and interest, that you feel truly cared for and, yes, honored as an elder.

A nurse's aide walked the hallways of St. John's with me at 3 a.m. to help me relieve the discomfort from the air pumped into my body cavity so the surgeon could better see what he was doing with the robotic arms. Up and down, back and forth we went, his arm around my waist, telling me what a good job I was doing so soon after the prostatectomy.

The youthful radiation techs at Minnesota Oncology not only carefully positioned my body under the radiation generator, they put a pillow under my head and pulled my pants down—but not too far—to expose the radiation site. They also shared a part of their life stories and asked me about my own. After eight weeks and 39 bombardments, we were like family.

At the end, they awarded me a Certificate of Achievement for "courageously completing radiation treatments." Best wishes, they wrote, and signed it Taniesha, Joe, Brian, Katie, Alex, Heath, Liz, Sarah, Kaylen, and Jen. I probably will never see them again, but I'll be reminded of them whenever I pass Minnesota Oncology in Maplewood...and get a sudden urge to pee.

When I think about my tangle and tango with cancer over the years, that feeling of fear has been nudged aside by gratitude. My reprieve comes six months at a time, from one PSA test to the next. It's a good reminder of how I want to live these "senior" years: one day at a time, starting with the one right in front of me.

A Member of the Board

I spent twenty of my years as a reporter covering councils, commissions, and committees. I was always aware of foibles and frailties I smugly believed were afflicting their members. I was amazed at how petty these people could be. I was amused at how supercilious they could appear. I thought them often intemperate, even infantile.

I believe I kept that out of my stories but not out of my memory. Thirty years later, after I was elected to the board of my townhome association—and had served six months—I was reminded of these old notions To my surprise, I found that I, myself, did not always rise above the fray.

I'm Thin-Skinned. I was weeding my little garden when a neighbor, in her 80s, approached me to complain about our lawn service. She said they were leaving ruts in the grass with the power mowers and she damned well wanted it to stop. "They cut the grass the day after it rained," I explained. "That's the day scheduled for our townhomes."

Why couldn't they wait a day? "Because they cut grass for other clients, too, " I snapped, "and we are not the center of the universe." I was angry and my teeth were clenched. An hour later I called to apologize. "I didn't know you were so sensitive," she said sweetly. Neither did I.

I Can Be Officious. As the chair of the Building and Grounds Committee, I was charged with delivering quarterly reports at the homeowners' meeting on our efforts to keep the property in good shape. I typed 'em out and read them with authority and gravity. "We replaced seven rotten railings," I intoned. "We repaved eight cracked driveways. We treated five trees for emerald ash borer." You'd have thought I was delivering the State of the Union address. I did not sound as though I welcomed comment or questions. I usually got none.

I'm Inclined to Worry and Wonder. Once a month, I'd wake up at two or three in the morning thinking about issues before the board—none of which were threats to the association's well-being. Did the homeowner who painted his front door emerald green in fact violate the covenant governing the units? Was it OK for a homeowner to put mulch on a hillside flower bed, as one resident wanted, or would it simply wash down the hillside all over the lawn, as another resident complained? These were important questions I'd never before considered in my 78 years.

I Can Be Resentful. One homeowner was constantly second-guessing my decisions and offering his solutions. I had to admit that half the time he turned out to be right, and that chapped my butt. When the board took an action that directly affected him, no one personally told him and he was offended. I knew I owed him an apology, but it took me two weeks to show up at his doorstep and tell him he was right. "I'm sorry. I didn't handle that well," I said. He was more gracious than I was graceful.

I'm a Sucker for Flattery. Friends and fellow-sippers in my coffee group tired of my complaining about serving on the townhome board. "Then get off the board," they said. "It's that simple." I think they privately wondered how valuable I'd be in a position offering more complaints than compliments, more anonymity than attention. They had seen my act for decades.

I told fellow board members on seve[...] I would be quitting when my first term end[...] leave," they replied. They told me they neede[...] experience, steady temperament (at board meeti[...] uine concern were valuable. Yeah, that and the fac[...] wanted the job. So, I'm now in the middle of my se[...] term, still complaining and vowing to quit. Unless, of course, I'm needed to preserve the good repair of the townhomes and the financial stability of the association.

I'm Not Above Using Political Spin. Some residents were complaining that the board was not moving fast enough with the landscaping plan to remove dead bushes, replace decorative rock, and plant new shrubs. I understood their feelings but felt the board was acting prudently and responsibly. So at the next quarterly meeting, I read my carefully worded report outlining eighteeen landscaping projects approved by the board and completed by the end of the summer. Some of those "projects" included removing and replacing a single bush, spreading some rocks, and filling a few holes. Before I finished, an uninformed observer would have thought we were competing with the University of Minnesota Landscape Arboretum.

I Have a Little Jealous Streak. I would regularly complain, as chair of the Building and Grounds Committee, about how thankless the job was: conducting inspections, noting problems, and checking repairs. Then one day a homeowner stepped up and volunteered to take over the job. Within three months he'd reorganized the committee, found more volunteers, established new priorities, and sought candid feedback.

Well, I thought, *isn't this special: Wait until he's been at this for a year and we'll see just how enthusiastic he is.* That was my first reaction. My second was to admit I was jealous—and maybe a little crazy not to be simply grateful. I am grateful for the few strengths I discovered as an elected representative of the people.

I Can Effect Compromise. Our five-member board would disagree occasionally about what to do, how to do it, and how to pay for it. But we were amicable, responsible and comfortable—with compromise. When we split over how best to deal with the effects of emerald ash borer on our trees, we eventually decided to treat some, cut some down, and replace a few of them.

I was pleasantly surprised how easy it was for me—like that tree in a wind—to bend a little. As a board we didn't break any limbs.

I Can Be Decisive. Sometimes the challenge is more about taking a stand than yielding some ground. I felt good knowing I could make a decision without taking weeks or months. I made some good, quick judgments in hiring a carpenter, picking a landscaper, and reducing our carbon footprint. When the county offered a small grant to help build an eco-friendly rain swale, we jumped in and got green. And when we hired the wrong guy to plow snow (too few plows, too many bad drivers), we blew him away.

I Can Be Empowering. Heeding advice from an old newsroom mentor that it's better to have people inside the tent peeing out than the other way around, I organized a townhome advisory group. The Building and Grounds Committee was to assist the board in selecting contractors, establishing priorities, and enforcing regulations. Committee members proved energetic and engaged. I turned out to be a good listener

Maybe I am ready for another go-around at elected office—perhaps a seat on my church council. That's right after I swim the English Channel.

Who, Me?

I thought I was being such a sensitive and sophisticated guy when I did my column for a seniors' magazine about a woman in her eighties and the short story she wrote about being sexually assaulted. I said the reason for doing the column was it helped me better understand the recent aggressive and active campaign by women against good old boys who abused, assaulted, and harassed them.

The victim's story, I wrote, shed light on why the memories of abuse could be so vivid, so powerful, so clear, after so many years—decades in some cases.

After the column ran, the criticism I got from both inside and outside *Minnesota Good Age Magazine* made me doubt just how enlightened I am. I was surprised over their reaction to what I wrote:

> *Then I heard a woman in her 80s recently read a story to a group of her fellow seniors about a night 60 years ago on a lonely country road in southern Minnesota as she was being driven home from a friend's wedding, where she'd been the maid of honor.*
>
> *She remembered the night with detailed clarity. The wedding went off without a hitch and was followed by a reception where people talked, danced and drank. As the party waned, the bride's brother offered to take his sister's attendant home, a farmhouse about 20 miles away. He'd*

been drinking but seemed all right to drive. On the way to her home, he pulled off on a side road and parked the car.

He leaned over and put his hand under the 19-year-old's dress. She shrieked. Her mind was racing, her head spinning, wondering what was happening — and why. She told him to stop. He didn't. Then, in a moment of calm, clarity and courage, she ripped off the wedding corsage from her dress and drove the pin into her attacker's thigh.

He let out a yelp, took his hand away and said he was sorry. He'd drive her straight home. On the way, he begged her not to tell anyone, especially her brothers.

And she did not. She didn't tell anyone. But here she was, six decades later, reading her short story to about a dozen of us sitting around a table in a 'retirement village.'

Her story of the evening and the unfolding event was as vivid as if it had happened a week ago. She read it slowly, softly, calmly and carefully. It was spellbinding. Now I truly understood. She hadn't been raped. Or threatened. But she HAD been humiliated, traumatized.

And that kind of experience does not go away.

Her story shocked and surprised me. I don't think any of the women sitting around the table felt that way. They knew at once why that night hung in her memory forever. I think sometimes guys, including me, tend to think: What's all the fuss about? Nothing much really happened — a wayward hand on the thigh, an unwanted kiss on the cheek.

The truth is, women don't do that to guys, at least in my experience. Oh, there was the sloppy kiss on the cheek when I went to my grandmother's and she hadn't seen me for awhile. That was merely embarrassing.

The recent revelations, recollections and reactions are more than embarrassments. What's encouraging is that our society has taken a step forward – toward respectful equality and soulful enlightenment. I can handle this new world, with its changing rules and rituals.

It turns out the 19-year-old girl, now a senior woman, could handle what happened to her on that country road.

She finished her short story with this observation: 'Apparently I didn't do any serious damage to him with that pin. He went on to get married, moved away and had five children.'

She smiled. The story was finished.

I thought I had represented my generation, guys in their 70s, with a heightened and enlightened empathy. Not so fast, came the reply. The first was from my editor, a woman I respect for her humor, integrity, and judgment. As usual she was polite to a fault in her email :

I had one internal reader who said saying that women don't assault men is 'irrelevant and a distraction' from the real point. I would have liked to see him write about what he and others can do in 'a new world.' She also thought you could have made a more direct conclusion in the last three sentences, rather than the fairly vague, soft ending.

The harshest criticism came from readers of *Good Age*. One really busted my chops.

In paragraph 9 you state 'She hadn't been raped. Or threatened.' Please note the following quotes from your article: '… a night on a lonely country road…a farmhouse about 20 miles away…He'd been drinking…He pulled off on a side road and parked the car…and put his hand under the 19-year-old's dress…She told him to stop. He didn't.'

How do you think things would have gone if she didn't happen to have a pin to strike back? How can you possibly say that she was not threatened? It is pretty clear to me that his intent was to rape her.

Imagine you are a 19-year-old man. Imagine a man clearly bigger, stronger and more experienced than you did to you what this man did to her. Go through the steps one by one: He's been drinking. You're alone with him on a country road. He pulls of on a side road. He parks the car. He puts his hand on your thigh. You ask him to stop. He won't.

Yes, I intentionally want you to imagine a 'he.' You can't possibly put yourself in her shoes by envisioning being attacked by a woman. I hope my comments help you understand why women know 'Men Just Don't Get It.'

This reaction to the column was so far from what I intended. I wondered whether I was ignoring some sins in my past with women I dated, women who were friends, women I taught at the University of St. Thomas or women who were colleagues at work.

I had to admit in my reporting days I spent more time worrying about stories than I did about relationships, and I recall being sometimes cavalier, callow and, maybe, callous. I could have done better— in some cases, much better.

With women who were friends, I did much better. I had a good set of boundaries. I showed up when they needed me. I treated them, I recall, with the same care and concern I gave to my male friends. And those boundaries applied to the women in my classes at St. Thomas. I believe I was a good teacher, a useful mentor and, more than once, a wise counselor.

When I was named managing editor of the *Minneapolis Star*, I chose Deborah Howell as my city editor, the first woman at the paper to have such a real, meaningful editor's role. She supervised dozens of reporters, photographers, editors, and secretaries, the majority of whom were men. I appointed her because I thought she was thoughtful, tough, tenacious and, when appropriate, tender-hearted. I left the paper proud of her—and my decision. (Howell ended her newspaper career as ombudsman of the *Washington Post*.)

What I'm not so proud of is a relationship I had with a younger reporter in the *Star's* newsroom when I was its managing editor. I'd been recently divorced and she was single. We'd known each other as colleagues.

She was bright, energetic, and dedicated to her job, but also seemingly carefree and curious. I thought this was kind of a fling for the two of us, with no lasting harm to either. But her career in the newsroom depended on the evaluations from her superiors, the most important being her city editor, Deborah Howell.

One day Howell strode into my office. She shut the door. "Nim," she said, "this affair, fling, whatever, is becoming a problem for me." She explained, tersely as I recall, that the woman I was dating was the same reporter she was supervising—and evaluating for future promotions.

"It doesn't look right," she said, "and it's unfair to her when the word gets out that she's seeing the managing editor. I'm her boss. You're my boss. You've put me in an untenable position. I want out of it. And you should get out of it. Now."

I mumbled something about the *Washington Post* and the long-standing relationship between its editor Ben Bradlee and reporter/columnist Sally Quinn. Howell grinned. Then she laughed. "Need I say it out loud," she said. "Do I really have to say it?"

No, she didn't. I told Howell we would end the affair and we did, without, as I recall, a lot of emotional anguish on either side. I'd been wrong. Howell was right. She was also more suited to the role of editor than I ever would be.

55 Years to the End of the Road

I pulled out of the Oklahoma City Airport in my rented car, heading southwest on I-44 toward Altus, 140 miles away, where my oldest and best friend was dying of pancreatic cancer. I was driving slower than usual, trying to figure out what to say and how to act.

Bob Lederer and I met when we were fifteen, and had shared a lot of firsts since that time: a double-date with girls on an Explorer Scout toboggan party, a bottle of beer on a lakeside dock, a L & M cigarette on a camping trip, the first day at Army boot camp in Ft. Leonard Wood, Missouri, and the first day of class at the University of Wisconsin in Madison.

We were about to share the first time we'd see each other for the last time. As I got closer to Altus, I found myself driving even slower, not wanting to face the last days with my old friend. But I'd promised to be in time for supper, so I picked up the pace and pulled up to the front door of Bob and Judene's townhouse about 5 o'clock. Judene gave me a hug at the door. She was the one who called me the week before and said it was time to come down if I had something to say.

When I walked past Judene, I saw Bob standing next to the dinner table, where three plates and silverware had been neatly set. It'd been only six months since I last saw him, but Bob looked ten years older. He'd lost twenty-five pounds, his cheeks were sunken and his skin hung loose on his face and arms. But he still had a smile for me. "Nim," he said, "you're just in time to get supper. Judene's not cooking. You're the designated delivery guy for a broasted chicken from the grocery store."

I was relieved I could do something useful right away. By the time I got back with the chicken, and some rolls I picked up, the two were seated at the table. Bob asked me to say a prayer, which I still remember because I thought it wasn't bad for the spur of the moment:

"Lord, thank you for the opportunity for old friends to be together. Thank you for the memories and please help us, teach us how to walk on this part of the journey. We haven't been over this ground before. And, oh yes, bless this food we are about to eat."

The chicken was good and so was the coleslaw and dinner rolls. I was hungry, but I could see that Bob was gamely picking at the small portions on his plate. Judene did a little better with hers. I helped clear the table and wash the dishes while Bob went to lie down on the hospital bed now tucked away in the corner of the living room. It was now becoming obvious he was too tired and worn to talk much, and I went to bed early.

Although I was dead tired from the drive, I couldn't get to sleep. I was thinking of all those times when Bob Lederer was at my side. He'd seen the highs and lows, the triumphs and trials, the faith and the fear, including the time he came back to pick me out of a snow bank on a sub-zero night after I decided to take a little nap on the walk home from the Hasty Tasty Tavern after a night of drinking on campus. He saved my life that night.

On another occasion he walked home with me from the hospital in Madison where my mother was being treated for ovarian cancer with a powerful drug carrying an ominous name: nitrogen mustard. She was shaking and retching that night, and I knew she was going to die; five months later she did.

On the way back to our campus duplex, we were silent. Every once in a while I'd brush away a tear. A block before we arrived, Bob grabbed my right arm. His grip was firm. I felt the power. I also felt the comfort. My old friend was with me. He wasn't about to let go.

I repaid the favor when he got back from his first combat tour in Vietnam. He was a second lieutenant in the First Infantry Division. When he landed at Wold Chamberlain Field in June 1967, tired and taciturn, I asked him how it was, and he replied, "No, Nim, not now. I want to fish and soak in some peace and quiet." I got the idea.

Bob Lederer and me

We headed to Ontario and for the next seven days we fished on Dog Lake, northwest of Thunder Bay. We fished at least twelve hours a day, catching northerns until our arms ached. At night we grilled T-bones on the shore and drank Crown Royal from tin cups. We laughed a lot, drank a lot, sat quiet a lot. Day by day, I watched my buddy begin to settle back into the world I knew.

As I lay awake staring at the ceiling, images came and

went. Over the years, I thought, Bob and I really did share handshakes and heart aches, triumphs and troubles, We knew each other's secrets, some of which we'd never tell another human being. Yep, he knew me better than any man alive.

We talked on the phone once a week for forty years. We fished together in Canada, with other friends in various combinations, for a week in every one of those years. No matter who was along or where we were, Bob and I fished together on the last day. I went to sleep recalling the last day of the last trip to Pickerel Arm of Minnitaki Lake: The sun was warm, the lake was calm, the walleyes were biting.

When I went down for breakfast in the morning, only Judene was at the table. Bob was still in bed, asleep. He'd had a restless, uncomfortable night, she told me, and she'd been up with him; by daylight he was exhausted. We weren't going to tell many stories on this day. No, the visit wasn't going to be about my needs.

I had to smile seeing self-centeredness still topping my list of character defects. By that afternoon, I got my head straight and let the day go as it would. That meant sitting in a rocking chair next to Bob's bed. After a while I could catch the rhythm of his breathing and rock forward with the inhale and back on the exhale. It felt amazingly peaceful and satisfying: in a way, rocking soul-to-soul.

I rocked away the next morning with Bob, too, but in the afternoon he found a burst of energy and we went upstairs to sort through his U.S. Army gear and memorabilia, trying to figure out what his son David might want. Watching him climb the stairs to his study was heart rending, but I playfully gave him a little push from behind.

We looked through a collection of pistol belts, helmet liners, canteens, backpacks, and combat boots. We picked out the best of each for David (a career officer in the U.S. Air Force) and then I spotted a small, flat box. I opened it and found a Bronze Star. "Damn, Bob," I said, "this is a medal for heroism. What'd you do?"

He smiled and took almost a minute to reply. "I stayed alive," he said. I pressed him for details but he offered none. That was the way he dealt with his two tours of duty in Vietnam. The only time I heard him even remotely refer to his experience was on a fishing trip. A bunch of us were talking about the atrocities of war and wondered how anyone could torture a helpless prisoner. Bob listened quietly to the raucous discussion, and then said this: "Don't be too sure, boys, what you would or would not do if one of your buddies was killed in front of you. You might be surprised." That was it.

Ron Handberg asked Bob on another Canadian trip whether his two children, Kristen and David, had ever asked about his war experience. He said they hadn't. Handberg asked whether he was ever tempted to tell them. He said he wasn't. "Ron," he said quietly, politely, "that was another lifetime."

Before we left the stuff set aside for David and headed back downstairs, I asked Bob how he was doing with his decision to only seek palliative care in his home hospice setting. He said he'd seen too many people suffer the effects of useless chemotherapy in the face of great odds. He didn't want that. He said he did not feel put upon by God or thrown to the wolves.

He'd retired early enough from his job as a legal aid lawyer to roam the country with Judene in a motor home. They'd been to Alaska, the north, east, south, and west. And everywhere he went, he found a place to fish. He'd lived longer than his parents, who both died in their late 60s; Bob was 69. "You know, Nim," he said, "I would have liked to make it to 75, to have another five or six years." That's the closest he came to a complaint.

The morning I left was tough for both of us. Bob had had another restless night and was constipated from the mild pain drugs he'd been taking. I was dreading the moment of leaving. Fortunately we got to share a moment that lightened the mood. I helped him to the toilet, clad only in his shorts. He sat on the pot and I rubbed his back.

"Damn," I said, "we've come a long way, haven't we? Together next to the crapper waiting for the earth to move." We both laughed. Five minutes later I helped him back to the bed in the living room. After I packed the car, I came back to his bedside. "You gotta know," I said, "you're the best man I ever met." He struggled to his feet and said it was the same for him.

We were even. I flipped the keys in my hand and walked out the door. I didn't stop the car until I hit the Altus outskirts. I put an Aretha Franklin CD in the player and listened to her sing "Amazing Grace," over and over, all the way to Oklahoma City.

> *Through many dangers, toils and snares,*
> *I have already come.*
> *'Tis grace hath brought me safe thus far,*
> *And grace will lead me home.*

The Dutchman

I first met Russ Krueger, the Minneapolis homicide detective, when I was a twenty-two-year-old reporter. The Dutchman, as he was known, was simply the best homicide cop west of New York City. And he helped make and shape my career at the *Minneapolis Star* as a young police reporter.

I first met Krueger at the bottom of a toboggan slide in Minnehaha Park. It was the Thursday following Ash Wednesday in 1963, and the body of sixteen-year-old Mary Bell was lying in the snow. She'd been stabbed in the back more than forty times; an ash mark was still on her forehead. It was kind of a lover's lane murder, a big deal in the 60's. Krueger took pity on me and answered questions I hadn't thought to ask. Hours later he arrested the guy who killed her.

This time around, I was standing on his doorstep on a Wednesday: March 21, 2018. Fifty-five years had passed, and I had come to his house in Long Lake to make an amend, to tell him I was sorry about a story that had run while I was the paper's managing editor. It mentioned him in an unfavorable light and I felt guilty, especially since he'd broken rules at least a dozen times to help me with a story.

As I waited anxiously for him to answer the door, I could hear him coming down the stairs, slowly, haltingly. As soon as he opened the door, I hollered, "Russ."

"Davey," he replied, and gave me a hug. He'd been calling me that ever since he knew my name. I always suspected it was because I was small and young and, well, kind of like a school kid in a suit and tie. The truth is, I not only didn't mind, I thought the moniker was kind of special – all right, endearing. I got that same feeling standing in Russ's house. I was the kid again. He was the old cop, bigger than life.

Even at ninety-two, his hair was still brown, not a fleck of grey. That's the way his father was, he said. It was painful, however, to watch him climb the stairs. I could tell it was an effort. He said he'd suffered a heart attack a few years ago and was now struggling with congestive heart failure.

"Sometimes I wake up in the middle of the night," he explained, "and I can't breathe. I pop a nitro tablet and that helps. I don't want to have a stroke. "

I told him that wouldn't happen and asked how he was doing day-to-day. Sometimes, he said, he felt like a prisoner in his house but was grateful a daughter was living with him, although he chafed at her cautions about watching his weight and his diet.

We made a little more small talk and then I got around to the elephant in the room: the amend I needed to make. Back when I was the managing editor of the *Minneapolis Star*, two of our reporters did a series of stories about the empire of Ferris Alexander, called the "reputed pornography king of Minnesota." Alexander was convicted of racketeering, obscenity, and tax fraud in 1990.

One of the *Star*'s stories, a draft of which I approved, quoted the head of the Minneapolis police morals squad saying that Krueger had approached him, telling him to "stay away from the Arab on the avenue." The implication was clear: Krueger was interceding on Alexander's behalf.

I winced when I read the draft but the city editor said the reporters had a corroborating source to the morals squad chief and I signed off on it. I don't think I ever called The Dutchman to tell him what was coming.

Facing him on the couch, I told Russ I was sorry, that I at least owed him a phone call. "Davey," he said, "Ferris Alexander and I didn't like each other. In fact he told others that we were enemies. I never did any favors for Ferris Alexander."

I believe him because I knew some of those for whom Krueger did favors. They were informants, and The Dutchman had more of them than any cop I knew. They were black and white, younger and older, straight and gay. When something bad went down, when Krueger was looking for answers or suspects, they gave him names and addresses.

Krueger returned the favors when he could. Most often he simply looked the other way at their minor indiscretions. One of those informants, a "snitch" in cop parlance, ran a barbecue joint in north Minneapolis and, in addition to ribs and wings, you could get whiskey and brandy in a coffee cup after the legal closing time.

The Dutchman Russ Krueger and me

I know because I was there two or three times, drinking with my fellow reporter, Bob Schranck, and with Krueger. I could have been arrested for being in a disorderly house but I've never been conflicted over that behavior. Hell, it was a place where people who worked as waiters and cooks could get a drink and listen to a little music.

Even during times of racial tension, The Dutchman had an affinity for, and got respect from, more than a few "brothers" on the North Side. What they found in him was street savvy, straight talk, and shared tastes.

One night after the fancy bars closed in downtown, including the place where Russ moonlighted as a bouncer, he brought a couple of guests over to the Cozy Bar on Plymouth Avenue for a nightcap: Jimmy Durante and Richard Boone, who played Paladin on television's *Have Gun Will Travel*. Durante got up, sang with the house band, and blew the room away. Whenever Krueger walked into Cozy's after that, it was "Mr. Krueger, how're you doin'?"

Krueger's sources were instrumental in helping the detective solve almost 250 homicides during his career; that figure came from a guy who ought to know: longtime Hennepin County Attorney George C. Scott. Krueger's exploits on the streets of Minneapolis earned him a reputation in police squad rooms from New York to Chicago to Houston to Los Angeles.

When I was a reporter at WCCO Television, I once called the Chicago Police Department to see whether they'd arrested a Minneapolis suspect who had reportedly fled to the Windy City. I was transferred to a detective who listened indifferently as I told him I was a veteran reporter who'd covered Minneapolis cops. "Do you know the Fox?" he asked, referring to another of Krueger's nicknames. I know Russ Krueger, I replied. What whiskey does he drink? Crown Royal. (So, there WAS some value in the hours we'd spent drinking.) And, yes, Chicago had the suspect in custody.

While street cops across the country liked Russ, I suspected the Feds in the Twin Cities were less enamored. The Dutchman was too unpredictable, too talkative (especially to reporters) and generally not the kind of buttoned-down, wingtip-wearing agents favored by the FBI.

Russ and I "shared" an experience with the FBI about six months after I took over the police beat. The state's insurance commissioner was seeking to restrain American Allied Insurance from doing business and to seize its assets because of irregularities. One of the company executives, Krueger said, thought the paper's coverage was slanted and unfair and wanted to set the record straight. Krueger made no claim as to the guy's creditability.

I agreed to meet him in the bar of the Normandy Motel in downtown Minneapolis. After listening for half an hour, I decided he had no case and I left. The next day I told the *Star's* federal courts reporter about my experience. The following day I got a call from a FBI supervisor, asking if I could come over for a chat.

Naively, I thought they must have heard about what a good reporter I was and were going to offer up a story. When I got to the office, somebody gave me a tour, showed me the ready room (where weapons were stored) and let me hold a Thompson submachine gun. Then, then, two agents appeared and said they had a few questions for me—in an interrogation room.

Did I meet with an insurance executive recently? they asked. What did he want? What did I say to him? For a moment I was flabbergasted. I didn't know why they'd care. But I had no trouble answering their first three questions: I couldn't remember much about the conversation because the insurance guy didn't make much sense and had no specifics on alleged inaccuracies in published stories.

The next question caused a lump in my throat. Who arranged the meeting? A source, I said. Who? That's confidential. Was it a cop, since you ARE a cop reporter. Yeah, it was. A detective? I don't think I can answer that, I mumbled. By now I figured I'd all but spelled out Krueger's name. I had been "played" and I felt bad.

That is until I walked out of the room to see Krueger and two agents walking into another. We'd been down the hall from each other. Together in his living room, Russ and I laughed about the experience which he called "part of my rookie learning curve."

When we'd finished with our stories, we shared some of our losses. For me they included a father, a mentor, a first boss, a half-dozen good friends and an ex-wife. For Russ they were former cop partners; Florence, his wife of 69 years; and a daughter, Kathy, whom he adored.

"She was a sweet woman who always looked out after me," he said, "and you're not supposed to see your children die. I'm still having a hard time with that." Especially an old cop who worked too much, drove too fast, lived too hard, and should have died thirty years ago from an aggressive colon cancer that required major surgery and seven months of chemotherapy.

Russ also left me with the impression he felt comforted by an abiding faith in God and His Son, whose grace The Dutchman figured would lead him safely home. This was a soulful side that I hadn't seen before. As I was about to go out the door, Russ got up from the couch and said, "Davey. Thanks for coming. You made my day."

"Russ, you made my career. I'll be back."

(I visited Russ again, two months before he died on July 6, 2018.)

What's Wrong with Your Face?

I slipped the landing net under a feisty walleye that Ron Handberg had just cranked to the boat. It was the fourth or fifth nice fish I'd netted, typical of the day I was having on Pickerel Arm of Lake Minnitaki.

It was the last week in August, 2005, the fifth year I'd been coming with the same fishing gang to fish this Canadian-shield lake, with its rocky shorelines, gravel points and spruce woods. We'd had many good days here in the past where the walleyes cooperated and we filled our fish bags.

On this day six of us were out, two to a boat, and as far as Handberg was concerned, the fishing was terrific. As for me, I was the guy with the landing net. We were both trolling with long-line spinners tipped with a leach. We fished the same water, with the same bait, at the same speed. I'd had a couple of other days like this with Ron—just watching him catch fish. I tried to be a good sport but my smile finally disappeared after netting his last fish. Always magnanimous—especially when he had a "hot hand"—Ron noticed my quiet despair and offered me his spinner.

To heck with pride. I took it and attached it to my line. It had a green blade. I put on a leech and let the line spool out; within a minute, I had a strike. I pointed the rod tip toward the fish and set the hook. I could feel the fish for a moment and then the line went slack. A northern pike had inhaled the bait and bit through the line. No fish. No lure.

No redemption. Meanwhile, Handberg was reeling in another walleye on a different spinner.

As we headed back to camp that evening, I put the hammer down and we fairly flew across Pickerel Arm. I needed a cup of coffee, some supper, and a new attitude. When I was a kid, you could pout over a day like this. As an adult, you're expected to show some grace. Getting back to shore alive was the most graceful thing I did that day.

I didn't sleep very well that night. My right eye was hurting, as though I'd caught a cinder in it; as it turned out, that was a warning sign of what was to come.

The next morning, when I went into the bathroom to brush my teeth and wash up, I looked in the mirror. To my surprise—no, it was more like horror—the right side of my mouth drooped, maybe a half inch lower than the left. I thought maybe I'd suffered a small stroke during the night, but I could move my arms, squeeze my fingers, lift my legs, and turn my head. But I couldn't close my right eyelid.

I finished combing my hair, went out to the kitchen table, and said nothing to my five fishing buddies. I wasn't the cook on duty that morning so all I had to do was eat scrambled eggs and bacon. That went fine. Drinking coffee was another matter. Because of the drooping lip, I drooled when I drank. Yet no one around the table, not one, said anything about my face.

I helped with the dishes, grabbed my fishing tackle, and headed to the boat. On this day, I was fishing with Ted Smebakken. Ted was a great guy but not always terribly aware of his surroundings. We headed down lake, having agreed to meet the others at a designated bay for a shore lunch of sandwiches, coffee, and soda.

Ted and I trolled the shorelines, caught a few walleyes,

and said very little to each other. My heart wasn't in the fishing. I kept trying to move the right side of my mouth. About noon we pulled into the designated bay and onto a flat rock, alongside the other two boats. I grabbed my sandwich and took a can from the cooler.

As soon as I tried to take a drink, the root beer spilled out of my mouth, rolled down my chin, and soaked the front of my shirt. Handberg looked at me. "What the Hell," he said, "is wrong with your face?"

So I was NOT crazy. As soon as Handberg broke the silence, the other four guys chimed in about my drooping mouth. We all decided to head back to camp, where I could call my doctor and ask her advice about what to do. Dr. Denise Long told me she suspected I had Bell's Palsy, a paralysis caused by a virus affecting the facial nerves. She said it disappears in a week or so in most cases.

I did not ask her about the other cases, but I did take her advice about going to a hospital to rule out a stroke. The nearest one was fifty miles to the south, in the mill town of Dryden, Ontario.

My old high school friend Bob Lederer drove me to Dryden. On the way, I told him—and I thought I was being pretty stoic and serene—that I could cope with whatever it turned out that I had. If the paralysis was permanent, I'd be O.K.

I was surprised at how calm I was. I wasn't doing television news anymore. I was retired. I could walk. I could talk. If I couldn't drink from a glass, I'd sip through a straw. Of course, I hadn't looked at my face lately.

When I got to the Dryden Hospital, they checked me in right away. It's single-payer, government-run health care. The doctor who saw me was on vacation from Winnipeg, moonlighting that day in the emergency room. He checked my heart and breathing with a stethoscope, took my pulse, and looked into my eyes.

Then he asked me how the fishing was and, for the next five minutes, we talked about water, waves, and walleyes. Finally, the doc asked me to stretch out my arms in front of me, palms up. He put his hands over mine. Push up. Now push down. Push out and push in—all against the resistance from his hands. The whole procedure took no more than a couple of minutes.

"You've got Bell's Palsy," he said, and he wrote a prescription for a steroid to reduce the nerve swelling. He also gave me a patch to cover the eye where the lid didn't close. He said the steroid might help a little but time was my best ally.

"Shouldn't I have more tests?" I asked.

"If you were in the U.S. you would have," he said, matter-of-factly. "They would have given you a MRI and billed the insurance company for $6,000. The chances are 99 out of 100, you've got Bell's Palsy."

On our way out of the hospital, I checked out the nightly news on a TV set in the visitors' lounge, and any residual feeling of self-pity I might have been harboring evaporated as we watched the CBC report on the death and destruction visited on New Orleans by Hurricane Katrina while we'd been out fishing.

Back at camp, in the cabin, we agreed I'd stay and finish the fishing trip. I was wearing the eye patch, had the steroid pills in my pocket, and felt a little better about my prospects. Tomorrow was another day and maybe my luck would change. I was ready for supper, but before I could sit down, Handberg looked at me from across the table. "Nim," he said, sounding sympathetic, "I've been thinking. If your face doesn't clear up in a week or so, I think you should find a Bell's Palsy support group."

He paused. "Then," he continued, "see if you can hook up with a woman who's afflicted on the other side of HER face. And you can take her to the Bell's Palsy Ball." The guys tried not to laugh but they couldn't help themselves. I tried to smile but I couldn't move my lips.

The Day We Put Gabriel Down

For the first forty-five years of my life, house cats and I rarely crossed paths. I didn't exactly dislike them, but they were a little too ornery and independent for my taste. If the animal couldn't fetch, or answer to a name, where's the fun? What's the point?

Yep. That summed up my feeling about cats. And then I met Kris. She had two of them—old black Ian and Spoons. Ian and I got along well. He liked to have his ears scratched and he was a talker. But Spoons, he hissed and snarled at me. The feeling became mutual.

Two months after Kris and I met, Ian died. She gave Spoons to her folks and they loved him. He didn't snarl or hiss at them, and that ticked me off a bit. After Kris and I married, we got a pair of Siamese kittens and Kris named them Ian and Tyson, after the Canadian folk singer. They were lovely little animals, and since we got them as kittens, they were extremely cooperative and responsive—more like dogs than cats.

I would pick Tyson up, with my hand under his front legs, and deposit him in a basket we used to store periodicals. He'd stand there on his hind legs, peering out from around the magazines. His brother, Ian, wasn't as cooperative and still possessed a shred of feline dignity. The pair were easy to be around, except that my allergies acted up; the allergist said animal dander was one of the offenders. Kris, in an act of loving generosity, gave the cats up to a friend of a friend.

My allergies didn't get much better and, after a year passed, Kris said that maybe we should get just ONE cat. It was hard to say no. Here was a woman who regularly visited the Afton animal shelter and came back with cat hair on her coat. I relented, and one Saturday afternoon she came back from the shelter with Gabriel. He was almost pure white, with a touch of rust around his throat and mane. His eyes were a bright, light blue.

At first he was nervous and fidgety. In fact, when Kris let him go, he darted down the basement stairs and found a hiding place in the suspended ceiling that partially covered the furnace room. That first week, the only time I saw Gabriel was in the morning when he wanted to be fed. He inhaled his food, and we speculated that his previous owner had been irregular in feeding the little guy.

Gradually, Gabriel and I established a relationship. He'd allow me to pet him and scratch behind his ears, but he determined when and for how long. Whenever a stranger came into the house, Gabriel would run for the basement. When I turned on the Shop Vac, he'd dart for the ceiling sanctuary. When he did sit on my lap as I watched *NYPD Blue*, any sudden movement on my part and he was gone.

While Gabriel was easily frightened, he was not beyond an adventure now and then. One day Kris decided to let him go outside, to roam the five-acre lot we had surrounding our house in Afton. I wasn't around when she let him out, but I was there when he straggled back home—bloodied, bruised, and bewildered.

Once inside, he let out a yowl to let us know he was hurting. He'd apparently wandered into the territory of a big, female cat next door and she clawed his back, scratched his face, and bit his testicles. Judging from the smell, Gabriel, in response to such savagery, had crapped all over himself. We stuck him in a laundry tub filled with soapy water, and while we were washing him gently, we noticed several deeper lacerations. Kris took him to the vet and two hours later, he came back with stitches and a couple of bald spots.

My impression was that Gabriel never looked or acted humiliated or defeated. He'd been roundly attacked, chewed, and clawed. But the Queen had only managed to mangle his flesh, not destroy his spirit. Nevertheless, we decided not to intentionally let him out of the house again.

Once in awhile, however, I'd leave the backdoor open a little too long and Gabriel would slip out and into the yard. I'd dash after him. He'd sit still until I got about two feet away, and then bolt.

"Gabriel," I'd say, "that's a good boy. Just stay there." Then I'd lunge at him, fall on my face, and watch him dart away. We performed this little dance a half dozen times. Gabriel would always come back to the house, but sometimes it was hours later. By that time I was usually frantic because I knew Kris was frightened Gabriel would get mauled again, or worse, hit by a car.

One Saturday morning when Gabriel slipped out of the open doorway, Kris was around to watch our catch-me-if-you-can act. "David," she said, "you've got to let Gabriel come back on his own terms."

"Yeah, well, what the hell do you think I've been doing?"

"No, you're trying to force him. You've got to *ask* him."

This I had to see, so I sat down on the patio chair next to the open door. Gabriel was fifty feet away, just staring at us. "Gaby," Kris said softly, "come on in now. You've been out long enough." He stared at her with that look of indifference. She kept repeating the mantra. And foot by foot, minute by minute, Gabriel moved closer to the deck. He'd look at me, look at her, look back at the yard.

When he got about ten feet from the door, he suddenly dashed into the house, pausing behind the doorway to look at me. It always had to be—at least partially—on his terns. His feline dignity required that.

He also seemed to have a sixth sense about us and our plans. I think he knew when we were getting ready to leave on a trip. About two or three days before we left, he'd follow us everywhere; he'd see us packing. On the morning we departed, he'd sit on the window sill and watch us put bags in the car. He wanted nothing to do with any goodbye pat; I think he was miffed.

When we returned, Gabriel's routine was always the same. Indifferent. Diffident. Oh yeah. You're home. Big deal. That lasted for about five minutes, and then he was at us constantly: purring, rubbing against our legs, anxious to be held. He needed attention. And, if you were so inclined, he needed to be loved.

I wouldn't talk about this to my fishing buddies, but it felt good to be needed. As the years passed, I got to understand what Gabriel needed. I was proud of the little guy for getting what he wanted. He seemed to understand my wanting to roughhouse with him once in awhile.

It happened gradually but one day we stopped the roughhousing. He was slowing down and losing weight. I remember the New Year's Eve when Gabriel missed on a couple of attempts to jump up on the arm chair. It was painful to watch, and I snatched him up and onto my lap. I wondered whether he'd make another year.

What never dawned on me was whether Kris and I would make it through the year. We had put together a real marriage–warm and loving—but in recent years our spiritual paths had taken us in different directions. I didn't think it was a deal-breaker; Kris did. By the time the snow melted, we'd agreed to part, a painful and agonizing decision after 18 years. The days were a blur: wanting to hang on, let go, stay put, and move on. By May I was the one staying put in the old farm-house; Kris was moving to a two-story frame house in St. Paul with a backyard and a flower garden.

We split everything fairly and amicably and Gabriel, of course, would go with Kris. I "talked" to him one night, told him Kris and I were splitting, that I loved him and I'd come to see him once in awhile in his new home. At one point, I couldn't help but smile: Here I was pouring my heart out to a cat. At least he had the decency to stay on the couch and listen—as long as I scratched his ears.

In the first month alone in the farmhouse, I can think of only once or twice that I opened the front door and didn't expect to see Gabriel come running from the kitchen to greet me. I went over to see him at Kris's and he looked thinner and more bedraggled each time.

She was worried about him, too, and took Gabriel to the veterinarians at the University of Minnesota who diagnosed advanced feline diabetes. It had damaged his organs. The out-look wasn't good, and Kris and I decided together that, when the time came, we would not let him suffer.

For the next month, Kris hovered over Gabriel, reduc-ing the carbohydrates in his food, checking his water intake, and generally showering him with attention, as she had always done. One day at the end of the summer, Kris called. She was crying. "It's time," she said. Gabriel could hardly drag himself up the basement stairs. We met that afternoon at the Feist Animal Hospital on Marshall Avenue in St. Paul.

The sun was bright and the day was warm when Kris pulled into the parking lot. She took Gabriel from his travel case, wrapped him in a soft bath towel and carried him across the lot. Travelling usually freaked Gabriel out, but he peered out quietly from the towel when I came over to scratch his ears.

I do believe he trusted us in that moment, that he knew we were trying to help him, to ease his struggles. Once inside the hospital, a vet tech took Gabriel into a back room to insert a catheter in his paw. Five minutes later, the veterinarian—a young guy with a warm smile—came out with Gabriel. He was as compassionate as any physician I'd ever seen.

He gently put Gaby in Kris' lap. She cradled him, I put my arm around her, and we said a prayer—and sat silently for five minutes. Then we let him go back into the vet's hands. The next time we saw Gabriel, the sweet, white cat was dead.

Kris carried Gabriel's body, wrapped in the towel, to her van. She gently laid him on the front seat, kissed me on the cheek and thanked me for being there. I closed her door and watched as she drove off, heading east on Marshall Avenue. I can't ever recall feeling so alone.

It's a fine line between grieving and self-pity and I was well over it, feeling about as sorry for myself as I could. I stood in the parking lot alone for a few minutes and then crawled into my car. I turned on the ignition and immediately recognized the sound of Willie Nelson's plaintive voice. The song was "Me and Paul."

> *"It's been rough and rocky travellin'*
> *But I'm finally standing upright on the ground.*
> *After taking several readings,*
> *I'm surprised to find my mind fairly sound."*

They were playing my song.

The Reporter's Daughter

When I heard on public radio that Erin Lee Carr had written a book, *All That You Leave Behind*, about her relationship with her late father, David, I knew I had to buy it and read it. David and I had a relationship going back to 1982, when I was a rookie reporter at WCCO Television. At the time, I was struggling to learn the craft of TV journalism after spending fifteen years at the *Minneapolis Star*. This ink-stained wretch found it wasn't so easy to become a blow-dried correspondent. Carr, who wound up at the *New York Times*, was then a freelancer for the *Twin Cities Reader*, and he was assigned to do a piece about my life and times on camera. He spent a couple of days with me, and the story he wrote was overly generous and gracious.

I met Carr's daughter Erin and her twin sister, Meagan, a decade later, after their father completed a residential treatment program for the alcohol and cocaine addiction that had overtaken his life and that of their mother. The girls were born prematurely, weighing only 2.7 and 2.9 pounds. David was to be their primary parent. Fresh out of treatment, he had an array of part-time freelance writing jobs, a supply of hand-outs and hand-me-downs for the girls, and a little help from the welfare machine. It was a rock n' roll ride.

He was closer to the front of the ride when I met him in November, 1982, in the basement studio of 'CCO on South Ninth Street. He looked like an unmade bed: hair disheveled, shirt wrinkled, shoes scuffed. He also had a charming smile and a pretty good idea of my background. He knew where I'd been, what I'd done, and why I left.

I asked him, "Why Me?" I was a little apprehensive about spending a day with a kid I didn't know, writing for a weekly that was known for having an "attitude." "Well," he said, "the editors thought you were an unlikely television guy, certainly not a hunk." He added that he'd heard some of my early reports and they sounded as though I was reading the phone book. "You've sure as hell improved," he said, and he ticked off four or five stories I'd done recently. I was impressed with his honesty, and his research.

Photographer Bill Kemplin and I took him with us to the cop shop where I had an appointment with the head of the Minneapolis Police Street Crimes Division. Lt. Bob Lutz was a good source. He told the truth. He knew a good story. He wasn't overly sensitive to criticism. Carr sat quietly in a corner while I talked to the lieutenant about a rash of purse snatches and wallet thefts happening on the Nicollet Mall in broad daylight. A lot of the victims were out-of-towners, some of them just stepping out of Dayton's.

I got some numbers, grabbed a sound bite from Lutz and then asked him where we could set up in a skyway—unnoticed —and watch the mall below. He gave us a location and said he'd tell the two plain clothes officers working the street that we were above them. Damn, this cop was worth his weight in gold to me. Before we left, I noticed Carr quietly sidled over to him and asked a few questions that I didn't catch. Both of them smiled, Carr closed his notebook, and we set off for the skyway.

For three hours we watched the pedestrian traffic, hunkered down behind the camera. No one's pocket got picked, no purse was stolen. But I did interview a couple of shoppers (who I thought looked like Greater Minnesota residents) about how carefully they'd watched their belongings. My geographic eye was perfect: One was from Fergus Falls and the other from Belle Plaine. Both were "shocked" that young thugs were stealing from customers.

We went back to the station, Kemplin and I agreeing we didn't have much of a story without pictures of a theft and an arrest. But it was a slow news days and I was going to fill a minute-and-a-half of air. I cobbled together the best yarn I could, accepting that our pictures were of the Nicollet Mall, shoppers, close-ups of purses in hands, and an interview with Lutz. As Carr said goodbye, I quietly mused about what in the world he'd write about.

A week later I knew. I was on the cover of the *Twin Cities Reader*. Carr spelled my name correctly, got his facts straight, and accurately reported the day's events. He also included an observation—maybe more of an opinion—that made me love the kid, especially that early in my television career.

> *When Nimmer quit as managing editor of the* Star *to work at WCCO, he took a big cut in pay and relative power. His colleagues doubted the wisdom of the move and his ability to pull it off. There were more than a few snickers around town. While no one doubted his news sense, Nimmer's physical presence wasn't perceived as a hot TV draw.*
>
> *No one snickers anymore. Nimmer has developed into one of the most effective news voices in town, and he has done it on camera without mirrors or wires.*

I ran into David about a month after the story was published and thanked him. He waved off the compliment but he couldn't shed his ragged appearance and trembling hand as he ordered a dozen chicken wings at the barbecue joint on

Fourth Avenue in south Minneapolis. For the next few years I lost track of David and apparently he did, too, a victim of crack and chaos.

When I learned he was in treatment at Eden House at 10th Street and Portland Avenue, a few blocks away from 'CCO, I paid him a visit. Eden House is a knock-em-up-aside-the-head program for addicts, many of whom did prison time and, like David, had been through spin-dry multiple times. In this place, they swept the floors, cooked their meals, made their beds, and obeyed the curfew.

When I walked inside on that spring afternoon, I felt like running away. The guys hanging around the edges of the reception room looked like they were planning a bank job. I put my hand over my wallet and smiled at every face that looked my way. I was relieved when Carr grabbed my hand and gave me a bear hug. "I'll protect you," he said, "but don't make any sudden moves." Carr would later write that a counselor once described the residents as "people who have been cut up, shot up and beat with chains. Some of us shot dope into our eyeballs because that's where the best veins were."

I came back for a couple more visits. Each time, David looked twenty pounds heavier. The place got free donuts, he said, from nearby bakeries. We talked of his hope that he could make a living as a journalist, and his fear that his infant daughters would be affected by their mother's drug use. It turns out, he need not have worried. The girls would do well in college, and he would cobble together a freelance chain, writing stories for business journals, weekly papers, and lawyer magazines.

My wife, Kris, was a lawyer for a prestigious Twin Cities firm and she marveled at how Carr could so quickly and accurately report the behind-the-scenes maneuvers at some of the bigger ones. I tried to convince Deborah Howell, my friend and editor of the *St. Paul Pioneer Press*, to hire Carr, but she thought he was too big a risk, citing several mistakes he'd made in stories. "Deborah," I replied, "he's writing twice as much as any of your reporters and he's doing it twice as fast. And he's a better reporter and twice the writer that you and I were."

" Maybe," she replied, "but we didn't have a drug habit."

As he struggled to land a full-time job, David got another blow to the head, a large lump in his neck that turned out to be Hodgkin's lymphoma. Doctors at the University of Minnesota slit his belly, removing his spleen, and irradiated his neck, killing the tumor. After that, he had a neck like a swan and a scar like a zipper but, as he said, it was one helluva easy way to lose weight. He also landed a full-time job as editor of the *Twin Cities Reader*. He was on his way.

Kris and I went to his house on Pillsbury Avenue one night to celebrate, the first time we met the twins, who were now four. Erin and Meagan played on the tattered rug in the living room while we set the table. David fed them mac and cheese and, after they went to bed, served us beef bourguignon. I marveled at how he dealt with the girls, never talking down to them, not raising his voice. He was good at this parenting stuff. That gave me courage to tell him I would be glad to take the girls Christmas shopping; they wanted to get him presents and needed a ride and, perhaps, a stop at McDonald's.

I picked them up on a snowy night, promised Carr I would drive carefully and we set off down Lake Street. We hit Sear's, a shoe store, and then McDonald's. The girls rejected my idea for a Happy Meal, and I recall at least one of them had a Big Mac. They finally found the present they were looking for at a small clothing store. In spite of my mild protest, they each bought him a set of underwear (in three different colors).

The best present, though, was the *Reader* editorship. Actually, it wasn't a gift. David's fearlessness as a reporter, along with a ferocious work ethic, earned him the job. And within three years, David, his new wife Jill, and the girls, were on their way to Washington, D.C., where he would be the editor of the *Washington City Paper*. It was the *Reader* on steroids, and Carr and his staff found plenty of targets for their insider reporting, including the *Washington Post* during its coverage of the Monica Lewinsky–Bill Clinton debacle. In 2002, Carr made it to the promised land—a reporting job at THE *New York Times*.

It didn't take long for Carr to become the best media reporter in the country. He could write about the bankrupt culture at the *Chicago Tribune* or cover the Oscars. His reporting was solid and his writing was colorful. He put it all together when he told his own story with a book in 2008, *The Night of the Gun*. In September, he came out to my Afton farmhouse with a copy. He'd heard I just had surgery for prostate cancer, and he wanted to make a personal delivery.

I was wearing a catheter bag on my ankle as we sat on the deck, looking over the little lake where I had fished with him and the girls. He plopped the book on the table. "Nimmy," he growled, trying to imitate me, "I paid for this copy myself since you can't get to a bookstore. Read the goddam thing right away in case you don't make it to the end of the year."

Turns out that Carr checked out first, collapsing on the newsroom floor at the *Times* on Feb. 12, 2015. News of his death reverberated around the Twin Cities; I was surprised at how empty I felt. I'd only talked with him a couple of times a year, but somehow he seemed a part of my reporter's DNA and I tried to make that clear in an email to Erin after I read *All That You Leave Behind*.

Erin, although I didn't see him much, David was always an inspiration to me. I've been going to AA meetings for 25 years and was sober for longer. But I was on that dry drunk: no idea of my defects of character and not much of an idea about how to live life as a grownup. You've learned those lessons and you gotta feel good about that. The man you admire and love – the one you wrote about – is the one I knew. And that makes me forever grateful. Keep writing and keep on with documentary journalism. The truth is more important than ever and must be told with grit and grace.

I never got a response to my email ; I suspect that Erin Lee Carr may never have seen it since I sent it to an address mentioned on her website. It doesn't matter. The gift she left to me was her book, her honesty, her insight, and her compassion. I especially remember the last chapter, which describes a trip she took to Alaska to fill a speaking engagement David accepted before he died. He was to speak to the Alaska Press Club.

His daughter filled in and even she had to admit she did it well. On her last day, she took a solitary walk on a glacier with a note in her pocket that she read aloud as she stood looking over the landscape and the snowcapped mountains. She was in the moment: no ear buds, no cell phone, no digital device.

"I don't have concrete evidence," she writes, *"that life exists beyond death, but I know I felt connected to him that day. I felt small and large all at once on that frozen wave. The glacier moves so slowly that the movement is impossible to register."*

I want a moment like that before I leave this earth. A moment I will never get is David giving me a tour of the *Times'* newsroom. He'd offered and somehow I failed to make it happen. So what I'm left with is the fact that Carr flew higher than any journalist I knew, including those with Harvard degrees and Ph.D's. He made it to best paper in the country and, not only that, he was a star there.

This is the same guy who opened his commencement speech to journalism graduates this way: "I was on welfare. I became dependent on the state for both food and medical treatments. I became a single parent at a time when no one would trust me with a ficus plant."

And I got to share a small part of this man's life. No wonder the thought always makes me smile.

It's Not on the Map

It was three in the morning in mid-March and I was wide awake in bed: no sleep, no peace, no perspective. Most of the thoughts that flashed across my mind—and a few that stuck there—had consequences I didn't like.

Ailments were stacking up. Losses were mounting. I get shots in both eyes every eight weeks for macular degeneration and I don't drive at night anymore. I wear a band on my right wrist to compensate for the arthritis. I'm missing a molar. I'm wearing a pad in my shorts to catch the leakage, the constant and collateral damage from the removal of my cancerous prostate. I've got to exercise every morning to tamp down the pain in my butt cheek and lower back. I used to get up and be ready to go out the door in 10 minutes. Now it takes almost an hour.

I can't stand on one leg anymore. If I were to get stopped for suspected DUI, I couldn't pass the field sobriety test although I haven't had a drink in 35 years. I misplace my glasses at least once a day, and twice a week I can't remember the name of some familiar face I meet on the street or in a coffee shop.

So what do you expect? I tell myself. *You're not the Lone Ranger. Getting old isn't for the faint of heart. You knew that. Now deal with it.* That does not, however, put me back to sleep. I think of the dozen fellow travelers I've lost in as many years: good friends, old friends, a first boss, a valued mentor, and an ex-wife who still holds a place in my heart and soul.

Then came the nagging questions—the ones that don't

have obvious answers, especially at three a.m. Do I have enough money to last me through this life? Will I wind up in a nursing home? What am I going to do with all my stuff when I have to downsize, hopefully to an apartment and not "the home"? And the toughest question of all: Why can't I let go of all this nonsense that is causing me to feel shameful about being so self-centered, self-involved, so into myself and my little life?

I do know how lucky and blessed I've been. I've never gone to bed hungry or homeless. I've got a pension, long-term care insurance, and a car that gets thirty-five miles to a gallon. I've got a host of friends and no obvious enemies. I have no right to feel depressed, deprived, or deserted. That's the rational part of me.

The emotional side sent me to a counselor, a Ph.D. psychologist at one of those euphemistically named "centers for family development." It's cover for those of us who don't want anyone to know we're seeing a therapist. The one I saw was a sharp-tongued little guy about ten years younger than me. I liked him and his straight-ahead approach. He told me I wasn't crazy for getting uneasy with growing older. He told me I might sleep better if I listened to music. I went out and bought an eight-CD set of music to sleep by. (It helped a little.)

He told me to keep busy, to do what I do. I told him I was writing a column for a seniors' magazine and working on some short stories. "Keep at it," he said. He told me to stop talking about seeing things perhaps for the last time. "You sound like dead man friggin' walking," he said. I got angry and told him I wasn't giving up, that I had a good life still ahead of me. "Then sound and act like it," he said.

Here is the most profound thing he told me: In this part of my life I get to be the "real" me, with the pretenses pushed aside. I thought about that for awhile and decided I was not the leader my teachers had predicted. I was a managing editor, but I was more comfortable as a reporter. I was an assistant news director, but I liked being a story teller. Nope, I wasn't meant to be a general; I was a soldier. What I was best at was comforting and connecting with my fellows. I knew what to say to those who were dying. I could get a group together for coffee. I could take a car-less friend shopping and help him feel better about his day.

That wouldn't get me on the cover of *Time Magazine* or leave a legendary legacy. In the end, however, these are the traits that come naturally to me, that best describe me. After a half dozen sessions with the counselor, I said goodbye and thank you.

A month later I unveiled my old-age struggles in a column for the seniors' magazine. I admitted I could neither escape the medical maladies nor resurrect the dead. But I could live the rest of my life, I wrote, with grit and grace. And then I revealed my plan:

Keep on Walking. For me walking is more than exercise. It's salve for the soul. It's aerobic. It's interactive. It's as challenging as I want to make it. I can hike to the bottom of the Grand Canyon—and scramble back up—or I can walk to the grocery store for a bottle of milk or a box of crackers. I can climb the stairs at church or hike to the post office to mail a letter. (How quaint that sounds in this time of technology, texting, and Twitter.) When I'm walking, I'm noticing what's around me. I'm saving gas money. And I'm less likely to be the instigator for, or target of road rage.

Keep on Listening. What I'm listening for is music, preferably live. Whether it's the blues at Bunker's Bar or Beethoven at Orchestra Hall, music can put a bounce in my step, a shiver along my spine, or a smile on my face. I can be lifted up or blown away. I was at Orchestra Hall when they played Mahler's Second Symphony. It was majestic. I was at The Dakota when Judy Collins sang "Send in the Clowns." It was nostalgic. Whatever the music, when it's good, it takes me to a place I can't otherwise find: sometimes hopeful, often joyful, and occasionally peaceful.

Keep on Serving. It's simple enough. Indulging in self-pity is well nigh impossible when you're helping someone worse off than you are. I'm no Mother Teresa but I do take an old friend with no driver's license to the grocery store. I visit a colleague in a nursing home. I write a blog for a nuns' website. I read short stories at a seniors' residence. And I do yard work for a few of those who can't. It is much easier to get out of a funk when you work up a sweat.

Keep on seeking. Since I believe this part of life is a spiritual journey, I've got to keep looking and learning how others are defining themselves. To that end, I watched a pair of documentaries on the life and times of Fred Rogers and Pope Francis, both men with strength of character and a sweetness of spirit. It was the Pontiff who had an insight I hadn't thought about in aging gracefully: 'A sense of humor is a gift I ask for every day.'

The takeaway from my collision with reality this summer is double-edged. First is that life is more fragile now. However, I am also freer and wiser now to be the man I always wanted to be.

I sure sounded as though I had it all figured out in that column , but in the fall, as I was pulling my boat on shore for the winter, that self-assurance disappeared with a pratfall. As I was taking the trolling motor off the transom and getting ready to put it on the dock. I tumbled backwards in the boat. I hit my head, thumped my tailbone, and bruised my back.

I doggedly kept on with the walking, listening, serving, and seeking. I really did. But life seemed more like an obligation than an opportunity. I tried to keep the feeling to myself since I'd promised my friend and partner, Cindy Lamont, that we'd go to Denver and spend the Christmas holiday with her sister, husband, and two grown children.

When we got to the Humphrey Terminal the day before Christmas Eve, I was pleasantly surprised to find the place only half full, as empty as I'd ever seen it. It took only minutes to pass through security. The coffee line at Caribou was short and they still had blueberry scones. I got the last *StarTribune* at the newsstand. I also got a window seat on the plane and watched as it climbed through the clouds and into the sunlight.

Maybe it was the sunshine—could have been the coffee—but I started a string of happy thoughts, good vibes, that flitted across my mind. They were people, places, times, and things that made me smile:

Holding Cindy's hand when the plane takes off and feeling loved, loving, and lucky.

Feeling the jolting first strike of the season on my bait casting rod from a bass that couldn't resist the Rat-L-Trap lure.

Finding the morning StarTribune *in my driveway, right in front of the garage door.*

Following that with the first sip of dark roast coffee, with just a touch of milk and sweetener.

Reading scripture at the annual Advent service and making sense of it.

Seeing the smile of an old friend with dementia as he spots me in the lobby of the nursing home. He remembers my name and doesn't ask me why I've stayed away so long.

Looking at the flourishing grape ivy that I ⸺
from a loved one who died too young.

Talking weekly with Andrea, an old frien⸺
who's a comeback kid on a giveback kick.

Noticing how good my 2008 Honda Accord s⸺ ⸺and
runs after I get the oil changed.

Maybe the answer to life's biggest question is in the small-est anecdotes of every day. And taking to heart that Serenity Prayer I frequently claim as my spiritual mantra but readily ignore in my weekly routine, especially the part speaking of living one day at a time and "accepting hardship as the path-way to peace."

I got a firsthand look at that "hardship" on Christmas Eve, enjoying a late-afternoon walk along West Alameda Park-way in Lakewood, a Denver suburb. I had just passed a small bus shelter when I noticed a man sitting on a bench inside. I heard a voice saying, "Help me." No, no, I'm not going back. He wants money and the smallest bill I have is $20; Christmas or not, that's not going to happen.

Then he spoke again: "Please, help me." I walked back to see the man, in his late 50s or early 60s, slumped against the back of the shelter, legs apart, a couple of empty 20-oz cans of malt liquor at his feet. "What's the problem?" I asked, sus-pecting the answer. He looked directly at me, speaking clearly, softly. "Alcohol. Call 9-1-1." I made the cell phone call, gave the location and described the situation.

I took off before the police arrived. But I did heed his call for help. Twenty-five years ago, I might have just kept on walking.

Goodbye Gift:
Forty Years and Still Floating

It was my last day at work at the *Minneapolis Star* after almost
16 years, and Barbara Flanagan and Jim Klobuchar, two
of its columnists, took me to lunch at Mayslack's in Northeast Minneapolis. The place served a roast beef sandwich—
medium rare—a little bigger than my head.

The lunch lasted an unusually long time, I thought, but
the three of us found plenty of stories to tell. The *Star* had
been the center of my life from the time I arrived as a rookie
reporter until now, November, 1978, when I was its managing
editor. I'd just got a new boss with new ideas I didn't understand. I was single. I had no kids. It was time to go and I had
a job offer as a reporter at WCCO Television.

When the three of us got back to the Star and Tribune
building, Klobuchar and Flanagan spent another five minutes
in the car talking with me. Promptly on the hour, we walked
in the front door and I understood the timing issue. In the
lobby, next to the giant world globe, was a boat on a trailer, a
Minn Kota trolling motor on the transom, and a hundred or
so reporters, editors, photographers, copy boys, and librarians
encircling it all.

They let out a cheer. I gulped and moved closer. My first
words—I'm not proud of them—were "It's a 'F----n' boat."
The scene was captured by a WCCO photographer recording
the presentation to the station's newest reporter.

In fact, the boat was a 14-foot AlumaCraft. The motor was a Minn Kota 55 (with a 12-volt battery thrown in) and the trailer was a Spartan. I still have the sales slips and the warranties. They are a permanent record of the best gift I ever got: generous and genuine, extravagant and relevant, personal and perfect.

A giant card came with the boat, signed by a couple of hundred donors and, within a month, I sent everyone of them a thank you note. But I never did know who organized the whole deal: collected the money, bought the boat and carried it into the building. To this day, I'm humbled by the effort and the generosity.

The boat gave a sense of closure to my newspaper career. Maybe I left some kind of a mark on the place and its people. Once I saw that AlumaCraft, I knew it was time to go. Fortunately I had a trailer hitch on my Buick. I spent ten minutes hooking it up and I was gone. I parked it for the winter in a friend's backyard.

The axle on the trailer eventually broke, the trolling motor wore out in seven or eight years, but the boat in still in tip-top shape: No leaks, no dents, no cracks, no sweat. It's been in use every year since '79.

The first time I used it was for WCCO's unofficial bass opener. Don Shelby and I paired up and I asked him to back up the trailer at a landing on Excelsior Bay of Lake Minnetonka. We caught some bass that day, and later I learned how to back up a trailer.

I also bought a used 9.9 hp Evinrude motor and took the rig from the Mississippi River to Mille Lacs, from Chisago to Crane Lake in Voyageur's National Park, and from Basswood, adjacent to the BWCA, to Bald Eagle in the metro. She was a boat for all waters, and for all sorts of fishing partners.

One of the first was an eleven-year-old girl. Suz was the daughter of an old friend—the only one of his three girls who liked to fish. I took her crappie fishing on Bald Eagle Lake. She sat in the bow and handled the anchor. She was patient and persistent, chatty, but not too. She baited her own hook, took the fish off and, most important, didn't have to pee all day. I took her again.

Another youngster was ten-year-old Will. He was already a fishing veteran when his dad asked me to take him along. Will could cast well, tie on a lure, net a fish, and untangle a snarl. What impressed me most, however, was his instinct. I had caught three or four bass on a rattle bait and Will hadn't connected. So I clipped off my bait and handed it to him and he started catching bass.

Before the day was over, we stopped along a shoreline to try for sunfish and Will had a small jig with a sparkle tail that was dynamite. He'd caught a half-dozen nice sunnies while I had none. Then, he clipped off his jig and handed it to me. No fool, I took it and started catching sunnies. I'm not sure that when I was Will's age I'd have been as generous. I did give the jig back.

The most unlikely, uncomfortable boat mate I ever had was Ken Davis, founder, owner, and director of Ken Davis Barbecue Sauce. Ken and I got to be friends after I did a story about him following race riots in Omaha that contributed to the demise of his janitorial service. Ken's idea of the outdoors was a walk across the parking lot at Byerly's.

He was a big man, upwards of 250 pounds, and sitting in my boat on Lake Minnetonka with his knees tucked under his chin, he reminded me of a black Buddha in the lotus position. We were floating low in the water, the fish weren't biting, and the sun was hot. "So tell me," Ken said, "about exactly where you find this 'spiritual experience' in fishing?"

I told him some days on the water were better than others and he shot back: "Let's get the Hell out of here and come back on one of the better days." That trip lasted one hour from launch to recovery.

The final fishing trip with my father in the boat lasted longer and produced a lingering regret. He was eighty-three, and osteoarthritis made it hard for him to hold a fishing rod, while macular degeneration had diminished his sight. It was a cool, damp, dreary day at the end of the summer. We were on a little lake near Aitkin, where a WCCO photographer had a trailer and hosted the station's walleye opener.

On this day, I couldn't find any walleyes, and I spent too much time looking for them and not enough talking to my old man. Fishing had been our real connection throughout the years, and I should have told him that. He took me along, whenever possible, on fishing trips with his buddies. I imagine that could have been an issue, with a twelve-year-old tagging along. The man who didn't have the patience to teach me to drive had more than enough to teach me to fish—and to love every moment of it.

This was the time to say thank you, and I missed it. He did know, however, that he was in a boat that'd been a gift from my newspaper buddies. I do think he was kind of impressed—he'd been the circulation manager of my hometown newspaper—that his only kid got a thoughtful send-off from a tough crowd.

During my time growing up in Fond du Lac, Wisconsin, Dad never owned a boat. We rented one from time to time, mostly on Lake Winnebago. Had we spent more time in a boat, I would have known my father in a more intimate way: The space between seats is perfect for a quiet conversation, of which we had too few.

For the last thirty years, my boat and I have floated on a little lake in eastern Washington County, a few miles from the St. Croix River. It's a fitting resting place for a senior citizen and an old boat. In addition to the scenery and the solitude, the only upkeep required is done with a sponge in the summer and a quick flip over in the fall. That's about as simple and satisfying as anything in my life.

The real value of the boat goes beyond fishing. It's a sanctuary. A lot of the time, my mind races, from things I did to things I need to do. Keeping in the moment is tough. But when I'm in that boat, I'm on the water. I'm with a friend. I'm in the only space that counts—mindful and peaceful.

When I look at that old AlumaCraft, especially when it's on the shore flipped over for the winter, I have to smile. It's a metaphor for my senior life: The rivets are tight. The hull is sturdy. The bottom is discolored by age and algae. But when you point the bow into the wind, she moves along just fine and will get you to shore.

More Than a Lake

The first look I got at the lake was not terribly impressive. Weeds covered the surface. The lake was small (eighty acres). It had no distinguishing shoreline features. The water was warm. Its color was light brown. And I was aboard an old pontoon boat with an equally old Johnson motor; the guy running the pontoon knew little about the lake, its fish, or its special features.

My wife, Kris, and I were considering whether to buy his place, a 60-year-old farmhouse on five acres of land and 150 feet of shoreline. We were there because we were about to get married and I said I wanted to live on a lake. This lake in southern Washington County, about three miles from the St. Croix River, was the only location we could remotely afford.

The owner told us he heard the lake had some big northerns in it, but he didn't fish so he didn't know how good the fishing was—or wasn't. He also didn't abide by the informal, accepted prohibition by the rest of the lake-dwellers on the use of outboard motors. As we chugged around the lake, I noticed a couple of other boats—powered by trolling motors.

No one was fishing but I couldn't help feeling that this looked like a bass lake: lily pads, a defined weed line, an outlet creek and some circles of sand on the bottom that might be spawning beds. A couple of weeks later, when I got a map from the DNR indicating a maximum depth of more than 40 feet in spots, I was convinced: the lake was good enough for me.

We bought the house, spent what extra money we had remodeling it, and moved into the place in April, 1987. I recall the Sunday afternoon when I'd finished the spring cleanup and asked Kris to come along while I took the boat out for the FIRST fishing trip. Was this indeed a bass lake or merely an overgrown waterhole for migratory fowl?

I went with one rod and reel and a package of plastic worms. I caught my first bass about fifty feet from the dock, and I went on to catch a half dozen more in the next two hours, none bigger than a pound and a half. "This is going to be a good fishing lake," I told Kris.

"That's nice," she replied.

"No," I said, "that's really, really nice."

This was the place I had dreamed of since I was a kid growing up in Fond du Lac, Wisconsin, at the foot of Lake Winnebago. Every chance I got, I'd go out to Lakeside Park, walk out to a little point that jutted into the lake, and cast for walleyes and northerns. My new lake was a tiny fraction of Winnebago's size, but in the more than twenty years I've lived there, I've caught plenty of northerns, bass, crappies, bluegills, and carp. A few of the bass weighed more than six pounds, and one of the northern weighed more than fifteen.

I fish better when I'm on my lake and, quite honestly, I've caught more fish each year. I know it sounds silly but I think the lake has been especially generous to me, and I've repaid the generosity by releasing most of what I catch, except for some crappies in the springtime.

I know it's spring when I see at least five separate shades of green around the lake, from the white oaks to the emerald pines. The colors just make me feel more alive, in tune with the coming summer—short sleeves and sunshine. Scattered among the taller trees are the smaller wild plum trees, with their delicate white blossoms.

My Aunt Orma, who lived to be 101 years old, used to tell stories about heading out to Afton and the St. Croix Valley to pick wild plums. I like to think she ended up prowling the shore of my little lake looking for those tasty plums. These days, of course, someone doing that would probably be cited for trespassing.

Those who do walk the shore in early summer will spot wild iris plants right next to the water. I have to look closely because the light lavender flowers are small and easy to miss. When I spot them, they are a constant delight with their graceful and delicate edges.

If Aunt Orma did walk the lake shore in late spring, she would have heard the peepers, those noisy little frogs with a mating call that's hard to miss—or ignore. I've heard them in the morning, in the middle of the day, and as the sun sets. They make a high-pitched peeping sound and it can go on for minutes—and stop in a second.

While it's easy to hear the peepers, seeing one is a rare occurrence, but I've spotted a half dozen over the years. They're no more than an inch long, tan in color, with darker markings on their backs. I am always delighted to hear them because their very presence is an indicator of a healthy ecosystem. I regard 'em as my habitat fire alarm and, so far at least, they keep on singing.

And my resident osprey keeps on coming back, with a nest high in a tree on a steep bank. I'll see her late in spring, with her white belly, flying overhead. She's looking for fish and when she spots one, well, I've been startled more than once when she hits the water like a dive bomber and comes up with a bass in her talons. One time the fish was so large I swore she'd never get off the water. But she did and she still does. Now, I tell myself the osprey is probably not the same bird, at least from years ago. And maybe she's a he. I guess it's the intimacy of the lake that keeps everything so personal and makes the bird a familiar friend.

The beaver that inhabited the lake for awhile was not friendly. Once, a fishing pal and I were casting along the shoreline for bass just before dusk. I heard the "thwack" before I saw the tail. Clearly, this beaver was territorial and felt we had no business on that stretch of water. I thought it was kind of strange since I saw no beaver house and hadn't seen a beaver on the lake for years.

But he or she stayed with us for the next three or four hundred yards down the shoreline, slapping that tail several times. If you weren't looking, it sounded like a rifle shot. That evening was the last time I saw the beaver and, to this day, I wonder what the critter was protecting.

Maybe I exhibit some of the same behavior when I refer to "my lake." Although it's a private lake with no public access, the water belongs to the taxpayers of the State of Minnesota. That's the way it ought to be and, at one time, I thought of giving a slice of my property to the DNR for a public landing. Kris talked me out of that idea, pointing out that whatever rules were to govern the lake would be only as good as the officers available to enforce them.

A DNR friend agreed, telling me that enforcement would be an issue since game wardens already had too much land and water to patrol. And without strict limits, the lake could be "fished out" in a season or two. So it remains a private lake—but not "my" lake. It's more likely I belong to the lake.

I kind of sealed the deal when I scattered Kris's ashes along the shore a few summers ago, after she died from lymphoma. Even though we had divorced, we always remained friends, bound together with memories of our place at the end of a country road.

The greatest gift the lake has offered me through the years is constancy: still small, still secluded, still serene…and silent. I've never heard an outboard on the lake, or seen a jet ski or a bass boat. The shoreline remains the same, with buffer zones of cattails and marsh grass between the manicured lawns and the water's edge.

In a world that constantly changes around me, from automobiles to zippers, the lake remains the same. It's a reference point for the life I've lived and what remains for me. It is small enough to wrap my mind around and be comforted. Although I no longer live there, my former next-door neighbor has let me keep my boat at his dock since 2008, when we sold our place. I still fish there, and when I need a sight for sore eyes, I come over for one more look.

These days, my old farmhouse is gone, replaced by a McMansion about the size of Cabela's, built by the developer who bought the land, which he is now in the process of rearranging, with rock walls and terraced flower beds. Nature's look wasn't quite good enough for him.

What is good enough for me is, when I'm in my boat, I can't see the place from my favorite fishing spots.

A Sunny Afternoon with The Bear

I first met The Bear about a week after I was made the police reporter for the *Minneapolis Star*. I was fresh out of college with a suit, two white shirts, a crew cut that was too short, a tie that was too long, and an eagerness to please anyone at the city desk.

My beat included the Minneapolis Police Department, the Hennepin County Sheriff's office, and the larger suburbs in the seven-county metropolitan area. I got off to a pretty good start with the Minneapolis police but I couldn't seem to develop any sources in the suburbs. I'd call out there and some desk sergeant would tell me that he "already talked to your night guy, Bob Schranck." That was The Bear, a nickname I gave to Schranck because of his burly frame, bearded face, and ambling gait.

It didn't take me long to figure out I'd better meet The Bear. When we met, I found him gregarious, garrulous, and generous. We were nothing alike. I've got more than a touch of OCD, with my shoes lined up in the closet, the hangers pointed in the same direction, the shirts, pants and suits arranged in neat clusters.

My desk at work was immaculate. The Bear's desk was once declared a fire hazard by a city inspector (no exaggeration). He regarded an empty table as a challenge. In a fishing camp, it would soon be cluttered with clothes, pipe tobacco, paperbacks, keys, eyeglasses, and maybe a grocery bag full of lures, reels, and assorted fish hooks (his makeshift tackle box).

I almost fell off my chair laughing when I saw The Bear on a sports segment of a KARE TV News show, talking about the necessity to sharpen hooks on lures before the fishing opener. I had never in my life seen The Bear sharpen a hook.

Bob "The Bear"

The Bear was married (and divorced) three times, and I do know that he had entered each union with the best of intentions. But The Bear's lifestyle didn't lend itself to marriage. For many years he worked nights. He had a Rolodex full of sources, friends, and characters. Time and dates were a relative concept and, often, he paid attention to neither. And he never met anyone with whom he could not start a conversation.

He proved that one night when we were out having a beer at some suburban saloon. The Bear had gone to the men's room—alone—but he came back to the table with another guy. He was boyishly handsome, well-dressed, and had an engaging smile.

The Bear grabbed the guy's arm, kind of steered him my way, and said, "Nim, meet Chad Mitchell." I stuck out my hand, nodded and said, "THE Chad Mitchell?" He nodded;

he WAS the Chad Mitchell from the Chad Mitchell Trio, the folk group that made the rounds of every major college campus in the country in the 1960s. When Mitchell launched his solo career, he was replaced by John Denver.

Mitchell was appearing later in the week at the Commodore Hotel in St. Paul, the old hangout of F. Scott Fitzgerald. After we'd chatted a little about the hotel's history, The Bear noted it was Thanksgiving in a couple of days and asked Mitchell whether he had any plans. He didn't, so The Bear invited him out to his house where he was "batching it" while his wife and kids were away.

The three of us spent Thanksgiving in the kitchen while The Bear sautéed thin strips of tenderloin from an antelope he'd shot in Wyoming that fall. The meat was tasty and tender, flavored with garlic, sage, fresh pepper and, according to The Bear, a touch of rosemary. Left alone, I would have fawned over Mitchell. The Bear did not and the conversation was easy and real, kind of like Schranck himself.

That's why he was so good at getting cranky and crusty cops to talk, especially when the chips were down, the TV crews were around, and the pressure was on—just like that evening in August, 1967, in Pearl Lake, Minn. The Bear and I were dispatched to cover the death of a woman and her four children in a farmhouse in the countryside outside of St. Cloud.

The first reports said that the farmer—the woman's husband and kids' father—was found wounded, hanging between two clothes-line poles in the yard. He reported that a band of marauders, four or five, barged into the house as he and his wife were watching a movie. They shot and killed his wife, shot him in the side, and set fire to the house; the sleeping children died in the blaze.

When the Bear and I arrived, news crews from all over

the state were running around, trying to piece together the story. I was as frantic and frenetic as most of them. The Bear, on the other hand, kind of meandered around the yard and found a little guy in gum boots, an investigator with the state, digging in the debris.

I quietly walked over and stood behind them, eavesdropping. The detective told The Bear he was suspicious of the farmer's story, noting that his wound was too neat and clean, missing any vital organ, and the ropes that lashed him to the clothes poles were tied in slip knots that the farmer himself could have tied.

As the rest of the "newsies" chased after the marauder story, The Bear and I slipped into the hospital in St. Cloud, just in time to see two detectives coming out of the farmer's room, one saying to the other loud enough for us to hear, "Did you give him the Miranda warning?"

That made it clear to us: The farmer had confessed to shooting his wife and setting fire to the house to cover up the crime. We wrote the story overnight and the *Minneapolis Star* was the first to tell the world that the farmer, and not a pack of strangers, was responsible for the five deaths. It was The Bear at his best as a reporter.

The Bear at a best as a senior citizen came after he suffered a heart attack and struggled with the complications from congestive heart failure and diabetic neuropathy. By 2007 he was in an assisted living facility, The Homestead of Maplewood. His life was further diminished when he had a second attack, this one on a Homestead bus bringing seniors back from lunch at an Olive Garden.

The Bear suddenly slumped over, his head in the lap of a woman sitting next to him. He wasn't breathing but he was only minutes from St. John's Hospital. That's where doctors chilled his body, jump-started his heart and, in effect, brought him back to life. It also left him confined to a wheelchair, unable to walk. He suffered from occasional spasms that caused him to twitch with the control of his motorized chair, once in awhile pinning a hapless nurse or resident against the wall.

Yet he remained cheerful, thoughtful, hopeful and, yes, graceful. He lived this part of his life with grace. The group that came to see him grew over the months because he was a joy to be around. We more often than not found him in his room, in the wheelchair, reading the *Minneapolis Star Tribune*. One time I asked him whether he ever wished that the doctors had "let him go," that he had made it safely and peacefully to the other side. I don't recall that he answered the question.

Several months before The Bear died, early in 2010, I came over alone to the Volunteers of America home to see him. It was a sunny winter afternoon and he was lying in bed, awake, but resting his eyes. I pulled his wheelchair over to his bedside and sat down, put my feet on the bed and leaned back. Within minutes, I was half asleep.

I woke up when I heard The Bear say, "Nim, I like it when you come over here and relax. You're like the brother I never had. And it's good to see you not running 90 miles an hour. You got to learn to take it easy."

Taking it easy was easier in The Bear's presence. I told him so. He told me there was no charge for the advice, or the example. And then we were quiet for awhile – like a couple of old dogs, grey around the muzzle, sprawled in the sun.

I went back to dozing in the wheelchair. I woke up again when I heard The Bear stir and say softly, "Nim?"

"Yeah?"

"I was thinking about the question you asked on how I felt about them bringing me back to life. If they had let me go, you know, we wouldn't have had this afternoon."

No Country for Old Men

My fascination with the Grand Canyon began when I was twelve years old. My grandmother took the family on a tour of the West aboard the Santa Fe Super Chief. Our first stop was Williams, Arizona. It was winter, and the burgundy, red, pink, brown, and tan of the canyon's walls, buttes, and plateaus were etched in snow.

I returned fifty years later for a brief stop and a mile-and-half hike down the Bright Angel Trail. This time it was spring. I could see the trail in the distance, snaking its way to the Colorado River, and I knew I had to come back and walk to the bottom of the canyon. It struck me as a spiritual place, like Lake Superior, designed to instill awe, or at least to demonstrate how puny a role we humans play in the scheme of things.

I came back in August, 2015, with Don Shelby, my friend and adventure guide since we met in the newsroom of WCCO Television in 1979. We've also been on three canoe trips to the Boundary Waters and a horseback expedition to Montana's Bob Marshall Wilderness Area. Shelby is good in the outdoors: confident, calm, and controlled—especially in the face of the unexpected.

I was not expecting what happened as we hiked down the Kaibab Trail toward Phantom Ranch on that sunny Saturday morning. I had just fallen for the second time, right on my tailbone, and I struggled to get to my feet with my pack and a gallon of water. I knew this wasn't going to be a walk in the park, not at our age. (Shelby was sixty-eight at the time; I was seventy-five).

The trail was rocky, steep, and treacherous because of the heavy rains the day before. You had to step down a foot or 18 inches in some spots, from a log into a puddle and onto a slippery rock. I had hiking poles to lean on but, after that second fall, I seemed to lose strength in the quadricep muscles of my left leg. I couldn't stand on that leg.

We weren't even halfway down the trail, and I was already feeling beaten and beleaguered. I called for Shelby, who helped me to my feet and carried my (and his) pack for the next half mile. As I hobbled along behind him, I was overcome with second thoughts: What made me think I could do this in the middle of summer—the temperature in the canyon's gorge reaches 106 degrees—and well beyond middle age?

I had spent four months preparing, training of sorts, hiking twenty-five miles a week, carrying a fifteen-pound pack, walking up and down hills around Carver Lake in Woodbury. But that's not the Grand Canyon, and this wasn't like the trail I remembered from my visit in 2003. My confidence was not bolstered by the several dozen hikers who had passed us on the trail—men, women, boys, and girls—some wearing tennis shoes and sandals, high-stepping from one rock to another with no hesitation.

By the time we crossed the Colorado River on a suspension bridge, I was carrying my pack again and discovered, if not a second wind, at least an extra breath to keep me moving forward to Phantom Ranch, our bread and bunkhouse for the night. Before we got there, Don and I sat down on a rock and had a heart-to-heart, senior-to-senior chat. He did most of the talking.

"Nim," he said, "if that left leg of yours doesn't get any better, you can't walk almost ten miles up and out of here. We've got to think of what the alternative might be. And you can't let false pride get in your way."

I agreed, and we continued another mile to the Phantom Ranch, where we learned that NOT walking out of the canyon would mean spending a couple of days at the ranch (probably on the bunkhouse floor since all the beds were already reserved), while we waited for a mule to come down from the rim for the one-way trip back to the top. The return trip would cost us each an extra $900.

The bunkhouses at Phantom Ranch were not fancy: four bunk beds, a toilet, a shower and a wash basin. But they did have air conditioning, and we crawled into our top bunks and let the cool air blow over our worn bodies. As our muscles relaxed, our mood brightened. Then I got a letter from my pack that Jim Shoop, my life-long friend, had written, to be opened ONLY when we got to the Phantom Ranch.

"Congratulations guys," he wrote. "You made it down as I knew you would. I wish I could have made it with you but that ship has sailed for these old bones. Just in case you might need a little extra inspiration for the trek back up, I thought you might enjoy these words from the guy who first saw what you just did."

Then Shoop added this quote from John Wesley Powell: "The glories and beauties of form, color and sound unite in the Grand Canyon—unrivaled even by the mountains, colors that vie with sunsets and sounds that span the diapason from tempest to tinkling raindrop, from cataract to bubbling fountains...

"It is a region more difficult to traverse than the Alps or the Himalayas, but if strength and courage are sufficient for

Don Shelby and me

the task ... a concept of sublimity can be obtained never again to be equaled on the hither side of Paradise."

It was as though the nineteenth-century U.S. soldier, geologist, and explorer were speaking directly to us. With the additional inspiration of a St. Christopher's medal from the Visitation nuns of North Minneapolis that was tied to Shelby's pack, we decided we would walk out of this canyon the next morning. I didn't sleep much that night.

We got up at 5 a.m., ate a breakfast of scrambled eggs and pancakes, and got prepared. Shelby wrapped his right knee (a torn meniscus) with an elastic bandage and did the same to my left thigh. It didn't surprise me his first-aid kit also allowed him to treat a snake bite, stitch a cut, or take your temperature (rectally).

We started our trek along Bright Angel Creek before the sun was up. The path would rise 4,400 feet in 9.3 miles before we reached the top. It took us fourteen hours—twelve if you take off the hour we spent at Indian Garden, the halfway spot, where we soaked our shirts with spring water, filled our bottles and rested our feet; and another hour at Three-Mile Resthouse, which we spent huddled with a dozen other hikers during a sudden afternoon downpour.

The wind howled, the thunder clapped, and the temperature dropped fifteen degrees. By the time it was over, small, brown rivers were pouring down the canyon walls and I worried the trail would be slippery.

That didn't bother a French couple who took off with their infant daughter in the husband's backpack. We followed five minutes later and were relieved to find that the trail was just fine. Shelby and I, however, were a little short of fine. We tackled the last three miles one step at a time, two switchbacks at a time and, finally, fifteen minutes at a time.

Before we hiked the last fifty yards to the canyon's rim, Shelby called a halt. Let's do it with style, he said, and we did, fairly sliding and gliding—looking good for no one but ourselves.

As I look back on it now, this trek was not for bragging rights. Shelby had already climbed mountains, carried canoes, run rivers, and battled the elements. And I can't brag about taking more than a half a day to hike 9 miles. No, this trip was for a better understanding of the life I'm trying to live.

I went to the Grand Canyon because I thought it was a spiritual place. It is. The colors are brilliant. The shapes are amazing. And the silence is overwhelming. I went because I'm alive, not ready to pack it in, tuck it up, or turn it over. I went because two old friends could once again share a trail—and a tale. We went 18 miles down and up and did not see another pair of hikers who came within 20 years of the 143 we had accumulated together.

Standing at the trail's end at nine o'clock at night, however, I lacked such perspective and purpose. Shelby had shucked his backpack and gone to get the car so we could find a restaurant and eat a late supper. I walked back to the Bright Angel Lodge to see whether they had saved a room for us.

I stumbled on the first step of the stairs leading up to the lobby, and the sharp pain in my right hip forced me to stop twice to catch my breath before I reached the porch.

NOT Just Lunch

The three of us—former DNR Commissioner Rod Sando, WCCO Anchorman Don Shelby, and I—were heading east along the Rogue River Gorge from the Oregon Coast in late summer of 2018. We'd just finished a fine two days, fishing salmon and hiking in an old-growth forest with lush ferns and giant redwoods. The most memorable part of the trip, however, was still ahead of us.

On the salmon charter boat we met a father and his two teenage sons from Boise, Idaho, and the boys were seasick from the time we left the dock at 6 a.m. until mid-afternoon, when we stopped to fish rock fish just a half-mile offshore. The boys, 16 and 18 years old, had hung in there, without whining or complaining, and were now catching the sporty rock fish (like a pound and a half crappie) one after another.

We cheered the boys on, and told them we admired their fortitude. When we reached the dock, they, in turn, shook our hands and thanked us for our patience. They were so polite and thoughtful I wished I'd taken a picture of 'em.

Shelby did take some pictures of the redwoods along the trail Sando had picked out for us. This was the northern end of their range and they stood among the myrtlewood, tanoaks, Douglas firs, and ferns. Shafts of sunlight cut through the forest canopy like a beam from a lighthouse. The trail was soft and silent, inspiring a kind of reverence.

It was easy to keep the feeling on the last day, as we began the thirty-two-mile trip along the Rogue to the tiny town of Agness. The silver ribbon at the bottom of the gorge wound its way through the emerald green of the canyon walls of Ponderosa pines , Douglas firs, and white ash trees.

This was a wilderness road, with narrow shoulders, one-lane bridges, dozens of S-curves separated by an occasional 90-degree corner. By the time we got to Agness, we were famished. We'd had no breakfast and were desperate for a café or a bar and grill.

We found neither, but we did spot an old, wooden sign on a post that advertised a ranch and fishing lodge. It was about a quarter mile down a gravel road, past a grass landing strip. The first look at the place took me back about sixty years.

When I was a kid my family often went fishing in northern Wisconsin, and we'd stopped for dinner on the way home at a lodge on the Wolf River. It was home to wealthy fly fishermen who stayed in its comfy rooms, drifted flies over the slick river runs, and returned back at the end of the day for a gourmet meal, followed by a glass of brandy, a cup of coffee and, I suspect, a fine cigar.

The lodge I was now standing in front of was, in fact, completed about 1912. It was a natural stopping place for people on their away from the Oregon coast to the railroad station. Prospectors, trappers, and fishermen stayed at the lodge and made the town of Agness their headquarters for mail and provisions.

The lodge was expanded in the 50s and 60s to accommodate guests brought up the river by jet boats. And until a few years ago, it provided lunch for adventurers taking rafting trips down the river. When we pulled up and parked in front, ours was the only car. I wasn't sure the place was open until I tried the front door. It opened, and I walked in.

The main lodge had a sitting room, hardwood floors, an upright piano, and a front desk with a guest registry. Some of the cabins around the lodge had names, all had numbers, and some had curtains and a stove. The dining room had long tables covered with red gingham tablecloths. They were empty save for a trio sitting at the end of one. They'd just finished breakfast.

Sando, Shelby, and I were standing behind them when the owner/operator, (a sixth-generation family member, I later learned) walked up. We asked about breakfast. She said she could make some French toast but it would take about twenty-five minutes.

However, lunch was ready right away if we'd settle for cold fried chicken, fresh biscuits, coleslaw, iced lemonade, and hot coffee. That'll do, we said, and we were eating in fewer than ten minutes. The food was fine. The waitress who served it was very fine—quick and efficient, solicitous and generous.

As she cleared the table, she spotted a tattoo on Shelby's wrist. "An Army insignia?" she asked. "No," he said, "my wife's name, but I was in the Air Force." She said her son had been in the Marine Corps, serving two tours in Iraq as a chopper mechanic. She was obviously proud of his service and subsequent college education.

But he came back changed, she said, and estranged from her. She'd never seen her two young grandchildren. She started to cry as she recalled that, in her family tradition, the children always came to see the parents. Not the case with her son. She apologized for the tears and we told her it was O.K. We were no strangers to pain.

Sando gently suggested that perhaps *she* ought to initiate the visit. And Shelby allowed as how he thought she probably wasn't part of the problem but could be part of the solution. I gave her a hug. She thanked us for listening, wiped her eyes with the back of her hand, and cleared the dishes. We paid the bill, left a tip and, on the way out, Shelby left another twenty with the owner to give to our waitress.

He said to tell her this was a down payment on a plane ticket to go see her son. She'd be happy to, she said, and then we asked her to take a picture of the three of us in front of her lodge. For some reason, we sensed this was a moment worth preserving. She took the picture, we got in Sando's truck and headed down the gravel road to I-5 and on to Portland.

For fifteen or twenty minutes, we rode in silence, just trying to process what had happened. The gift we'd been given was the sense that we could be trusted. We were left feeling wiser than we used to be: We listened better, talked less, and shared more. We gave suggestions, not directives. When Sando brought up a Bob Dylan track on the truck stereo, I was put in mind of lyrics to his "It's Alright, Ma":

> *You lose yourself, you reappear*
> *You suddenly find you got nothing to fear*
> *Alone you stand with nobody near*
> *When a trembling distant voice, unclear*
> *Startles your sleeping ears to hear*
> *That somebody thinks they really found you*

As we rolled later that day along the Rogue in the afternoon sun, it was clear that what we paid for, and what we got, was a helluva lot more than lunch.

The Replacements

During a coffee klatch with some of my old friends I mentioned having dinner with some of the students who'd been in the first classes I taught at the University of St. Thomas in the 90's. One of the guys asked whether this was a regular event and I said it was.

"Yes," I said, "I'm courting replacements for that old gang of mine. You guys keep droppin' like flies." We all chuckled, though I'll admit the remark bordered on the insensitive. But the truth is that in the previous decade I'd lost ten friends—men and women I was close to, who had shared life's trials, tribulations, and triumphs with me. Some died suddenly, with no chance for a goodbye. Others died slowly, which gave us time to say the important things to each other.

A lot of my friends have kids and grandkids to occupy those empty spaces. I do not, and that's why the former students are such a blessing. As I approach eighty, they're closing in on fifty, and those thirty years give me a shot of adrenaline, blasphemy, and courage. They are multi tasking, quick thinking, and fast moving. They juggle tasks in an hour that would take me a week.

What distinguishes them most, however, is their decency and generosity. They reached out to me after they graduated. They organized the dinners or get-togethers. And sometimes, they came to pick me up at my front door. The lives they've lived since I met them exhibit attributes that I first spotted in class.

And it's no exaggeration to say I find them helpful in my journey. Now I'm the seeker, the aging student in search of fresh manifestations of some old virtues. All I have to do is think of the name or see the face and the character of the "kid" takes shape and comes alive:

BAIRD: He spent his first year in college at the University of Minnesota. In his second year, I saw him on the staff of the student newspaper at St. Thomas, a reporter by instinct: curious, skeptical, savvy, and competitive. He came ready to "prime the pump," dropping a tidbit of gossip to a source he hoped would provide more than that in return.

Now he's the editor of a metro daily, working all hours, honing his skills, but first loving his family. He can throw a fly line in a graceful arc, catch his share of trout or bass, and carry my trolling battery to the boat. His father was one of my best friends.

BRIAN: From the first week Brian came to class, he sat around the table with his glass half full. He had an unbridled sense of optimism and it was catching. As an editor of the student newspaper, he put together a staff, got them to believe in the mission, and helped them to do their best work. As the paper's adviser, I was grateful Brian had the reins. All I had to do was hop aboard the wagon.

He and his wife now run their own business, raise a family, and find time to be volunteers. Hearing his voice cheers me up and on; he makes it sound as though I'm the most important person on his agenda. That's not bad when your best claim to fame is that you used to be somebody.

CHARLIE: He came to St. Thomas with the insight and integrity to find out who he really was and what he was about, and he did it with a quiet confidence that impressed me. When he

A few of the Replacements: (from left) Kathleen Hennessy, Brian Bellmont, Dave Aeikens, and me

got out of school, he went to a small town, stuck to his principles, followed his game, and learned his craft.

He came back to the Twin Cities for a heavy-hitting job that requires savvy, sensibility and, sometimes, silence. He manages all of that like a veteran, and he has one more "s" attribute I admire: serenity. He does not rattle easily.

DAVID: Dave had a sense of duty and dedication to the journalistic craft that put mine to shame when I was his age. From the first day he walked into my class, he was a newsman. He understood public affairs, he enjoyed the competition, he relished the responsibility. And I believe he could hear the "Battle Hymn of the Republic" in the background when anyone talked about journalism.

For two decades he reported, edited, and served as the president of a national news organization dedicated to ethics and truth telling. I am certain David never knowingly faked any facts or took any shortcuts. He was a journalistic Boy Scout who now has found a career that gives him more free time and space. He served his hitch on the front lines.

DYMANH: This Cambodian immigrant was in a special high school program at St. Thomas. At the age of seventeen, he had a purpose and passion that belied his youth. I've never seen anyone as enthusiastic, sometimes in the face of daunting odds.

I recall walking with Dymanh across the University of Minnesota campus on a sunny summer afternoon, declaring his intention to major in journalism. What a courageous move, I thought, for a refugee with English as a second language. I was more than a little overwhelmed. He was undeterred and undaunted. Today he's a television news photographer, with a wife and two children—and the same infectious smile.

IFRAH: Ifrah was, for me, the definition of courage. The Somali immigrant came to Minnesota alone, hardly speaking a word of English. She graduated from Roosevelt High School in Minneapolis, won a scholarship to St. Thomas, and toughed out four years to earn a degree in the liberal arts.

I remember her voicemails at 2:30 in the morning, asking for help in understanding a history text or interpreting a Bible verse for a religion course on the New Testament. In Somalia, she was the family goat herder. In St. Paul, she was the college student, the cafeteria worker, the dormitory roommate, and the only Muslim on her floor.

KATHLEEN: What I noticed about her as the semester ended was this finely tuned sense of balance she had in her life; she always knew where the fulcrum was. She could study, work, play, and protect, and she seemed to know when each was appropriate.

She carried on that ability to multi-task. After graduating, she worked in a broadcast newsroom, ran a division of a PR agency, raised a family, supported her girls' athletic teams, and found time to sing in a rock n' roll cover band. (I get anxious when I have two appointments in the same day.)

LAURA: She was a recent Minneapolis high school grad when I met her at a journalism camp at St. Thomas. She said she wanted to be a broadcast reporter, to learn about the craft of writing and interviewing. She was a quick study and a delight in class and had an instinctual feel for the human condition.

After she graduated from college, she became a crack TV reporter, survived some tough times (the kind that leave you on one knee sucking for air), bought a house, raised four kids and always sent me home with a sandwich when I came to visit.

MILES: He was a senior at St. Thomas when we first crossed paths; he worked with photo chief Brad Jacobsen and me on videos and the kid's work ethic impressed even an old warhorse like me. He'd get up at four in the morning to join us on a shoot. He'd carry the gear, let me sit in the front seat and tell me to watch out for an icy sidewalk.

Now he works for an international corporation and serves as kind of an unofficial advisor on diversity issues. He's walked soulfully and honestly between cultures and colors, always staying true to who he is and what he believes.

PAT: He was calm and quiet around me when he was a reporter on the student newspaper. At first I thought he might lack the competitive drive to survive in a newsroom. I learned that he had the drive. He just didn't get rattled. And he didn't need the constant reassurance some of us sought when we were younger.

He was a low-maintenance kid who did his job. And he continued to do that, from his first days as a reporter in the hinterland to his last as an editor in the metro heartland. He teaches me something about the nature of humility.

REBECCA: Before she left St. Thomas, Rebecca grew to be

feisty and fearless. She was determined to take care of herself, get answers to her questions, be skeptical of authority, and seek redress of her grievances. I enjoyed jousting with her.
She's worked for several employers, and each time she moved, she got a better job. In her large family, she's the aunt with the answers, the one you go to for straight talk, unquestioned support, and loving loyalty.

MY RELATIONSHIP WITH three of the students–Brian, David, and Kathleen—began in the first class I taught at St. Thomas: Writing for Broadcast. The trio read the book, watched the news, wrote their stories, and started lively discussions. They were a rookie teacher's best friend. And they did even more. At the end of the semester, they lugged around a petition, seeking to nominate me for Professor of the Year. The idea was patently ridiculous but they got enough signatures to put me on the ballot. They knew I didn't come from a traditional background in academe and I suspect they wanted to see that I got off to a fast start. That thoughtfulness was not in my playbook when I was their age.

At my age, I'm under no illusion that "the replacements" will fill the void left by the death of old friends. Like those old friends, they are neither perfect nor pure. But they are vigorous and vital and they give me a perspective that no others can.

They do not talk of pre-existing conditions, estate plans, or retirement portfolios. They inhabit a world where everything is still possible, and they are a constant reminder that the world is not going to hell in a hand basket.

Most of all, they're willing to befriend a man old enough to be their father. And solicitous enough to do it with one who is neither on Twitter nor Instagram.

An Honorary Nun

August 19, 2002, and my wife, Kris, and I were sitting at the dinner table of the Visitation Monastery of Minneapolis, a house on Fremont Avenue, about to have a meal with the six Sisters who made their ministry on the streets in the neighborhood of North Minneapolis.

It had been a rock n' roll ride for them since they moved into the house in 1989. Over the years they'd ministered to a drug dealer who got shot and left to die on their front lawn, gave music lessons to hundreds of children, read books to more than that, organized retreat and support groups for single mothers, made sandwiches for the homeless, prayed with and for the hopeless, and gave bus tokens to the carless.

On this evening, before supper, the good Sisters made me an honorary nun, giving me their Cross of Affiliation for my service to the ministry. It'll be my lifetime achievement and, for one of the few times in my life, I cried. It didn't last long, but tears did run down my cheeks.

I think I knew these women had been responsible for whatever spiritual life I had. They were and are for me, the closest I can come to imagining the God of my understanding on this earth and in this life. I got my first look in 1985 when, as a reporter for WCCO Television news, I went out to the Visitation Monastery in Mendota Heights with photographer Gordie Bartusch to do a story about the forty-some sisters who lived and prayed in this tranquil suburban setting.

Some had taught at Visitation High School and one, Sister Mary Frances Reis, quickly grabbed my attention and touched my heart. I asked her what the monastic life was about. She replied, " to serve God and Live Jesus."

"I do that in my way," she said, "and you do it in yours. We are all called to live holy lives." She talked about the "little virtues" of kindness and gentleness. "Be who you are and be that well," said her patron saint Francis de Sales.

From the very beginning, Mary Frances welcomed me to whatever holy ground she was standing upon. I just felt she thought I was a good man and, yet, she hardly knew me. But after we did the television story, Gordie and I returned to the monastery to have supper with the nuns. Here we were, a couple of news reprobates, breaking bread with the women who baked the bread.

When Kris and I decided to get married, I again went to the Mendota monastery to have her meet Mary Frances and some of the other Sisters who, as I recall, formed kind of a Sufi circle and blessed our impending union. For some damn reason, I wanted the women to know and be a part of the life ahead of me.

Kris and I did marry on November 15, 1986, and for the next couple of years I kind of lost track of the Visitation. I also lost sight of any semblance of a spiritual life. Kris and I were married in a little Lutheran church but I never went there again. I evaded my father's questions about a religious life. I know that hurt him, and it didn't make me feel real good telling him white lies about going to church.

I was the prodigal son wandering in the wilderness when, out of the blue one early spring day in 1989, Mary Frances called. I had decided to quit my reporting job at WCCO and go to the University of St. Thomas to teach journalism. It was an uneasy time and I felt relieved to hear the Sister's voice. "Dave," she said, "I'm joining three other Sisters from St. Louis to start an 'urban monastery' somewhere in the Twin Cities."

The idea, she explained, was to be a powerful, spiritual presence in a troubled neighborhood, one where gangs, guns, drugs and despair might be constant companions. And the Sisters would like me to be on their board of directors. Without hesitating, I said yes, and then I told Mary Frances I hoped they'd choose North Minneapolis as their hallowed ground.

After weeks of discernment, the Sisters—Mary Frances, Mary Margaret McKenzie, Mary Virginia Schmidt, and Karen Mohan—decided the north side was where they belonged, and they made plans to buy a house at 1527 Fremont Avenue. But before they could move in, they'd need a special use permit from the Minneapolis City Council because they were four unrelated adults who'd be living in a home designated for a single family.

It was in July when Mary Frances and I walked into a morning meeting of the council's Zoning and Planning Committee to make the case for an exception. I was no longer a reporter so I could choose a side, get involved. I'd never appeared before a government body before, although I'd covered plenty.

And I didn't get to appear that day, either, because the committee had a stacked agenda and didn't get around to the Fremont house. But Committee Chair Sharon Sayles Belton promised we'd get our chance the next day – first on the agenda. And we were. Mary Frances, I recall, talked about their mission and how much they wanted to be a part of the Northside. She was considerate, committed, compassionate, and, well, convincing.

I told the committee I thought the four nuns were more

My ex-wife Kris, Sister Mary Frances Reis, and me

a family than most. They prayed together. They ate together. They were used to living in close quarters. "Besides," I said, "the house they want to live in is deserted and dilapidated. They'll fix it up, plant a garden, open the back door and welcome the neighbors. That," I concluded, "sounds like a good deal for the city."

Then, according to Mary Frances, I uttered this final sentence: "And I'm not even a goddamn Catholic." I don't recall saying that, but if I did, I'm not proud of it. I am sometimes given to a bit of profane punctuation. This might have been one of those times.

The Sisters got their permit. They bought the house, fixed it up, and officially moved in on November, 11, 1989. Eventually they bought and remodeled a second house at 1619 Girard Avenue and split the monastery. Over the years, I've been at those houses hundreds of times.

I've chanted Psalms with the Sisters. I've attended their monthly neighborhood meetings. I've written profiles of their friends and neighbors. I've posted blogs on their website. I've delivered their Thanksgiving dinners. I've driven them to and from their fall retreats. I've contributed to their annual fund. And I've left them an estate gift.

And, yet, I am still in their debt. They are the stitching in whatever spiritual fabric I have in my life. They show me how to live the life I want—not because they're perfect but because they're persistent. They are anything but naïve. They can spot a con or a phony a mile away. They are acutely aware of their flaws and foibles. Maybe that's why I feel so drawn to them.

In the face of troubles and tragedies, they try to show gentleness and kindness. When Kris and I split up after eighteen years of marriage, I came running to the Sisters for comfort—to the original four: Frances, Virginia, Margaret and Karen. I wanted them to know we had tried to hold it together in spite of our very different spiritual paths. I wanted them to know I still loved her. I wanted them to know I could use a blessing.

The Sisters knew Kris well since we'd spent our Christmas Eves with them and attended their special events. After I told my story, they didn't choose sides or offer recriminations. They just held my hand, said they shared my pain and would offer a prayer—for both of us. I left their house that day feeling less like a failure and a little more like a survivor.

I've sometimes struggled with survivors, especially if I tried to help them, getting impatient if things didn't get better. Betty, the welfare mother who used to live near the Sisters, was a prime example. She'd been one of the subjects in a documentary I worked on about the effects of poverty and the difficulty in finding a way out. I figured I owed her.

So, for four or five years, I paid to store her furniture, bought her groceries, and tried to help her son get back into high school. She showed little progress. She still smoked crack. She was occasionally homeless. Old boyfriends still abused her. And she lost the job I arranged because she was frequently late for work.

I told Mary Frances I was frustrated and fed up, that Betty was hopeless and hapless. Frances gave me a stern look. "Dave," she said, "you're not her savior. Be her companion. Sit with her. Listen to her. Just be with her, and let that be enough."

I'm not sure I could ever see the face of Christ in Betty but I did see a different side. She was in a nursing home, dying of bone cancer, when I last saw her in 2008. It was the day before my surgery to remove a cancerous prostate gland. I had bought Betty a pack of her favorite cigarettes—Benson and Hedges Menthol 100s—and told her to light two. What the hell, I thought, tomorrow I could die.

So we sat on the lawn, Betty in her wheelchair and I on the grass, and smoked. I told her about the surgery and suggested she might say a prayer for me. She nodded but said nothing. When we finished the smokes, I got up, said goodbye and walked to my car. As I climbed in I heard her voice: "I love you, Dave." That's it, the last words from this mother of four, frequently a homeless crack addict. The same one I often wanted to write off, and out of my life.

I'm not as judgmental as I used to be, more inclined these days to tolerance than tirades. The Visitation nuns have set a good example. (Today the four are seven. Katherine Mullin, Suzanne Homeyer, and Brenda Lisenby have joined the founding Sisters.) The numbers have changed but their houses have ALWAYS been open to everyone: black and white, straight and gay, neighbor and suburbanite, rich and poor, priest and penitent, religious and reluctant. When I, a Lutheran, am at a

Mass at the monastery, the cup and the bread are given to me.

A few years ago, one of their neighbors was a drug addict and a sometimes dealer. The Sisters knew, and he knew they knew, and yet they had a real relationship. They prayed for him and he shoveled their walk and put up the Christmas tree. He was streetwise and savvy, born and raised in Chicago. I always suspected he put out the word on the street not to mess with the nuns. When he died, they were at his funeral, and his former wife is a close friend.

The Sisters could always walk the line between saints and sinners, offering the same charity on both sides. One early summer morning following a drug bust in the neighborhood, they served lemonade to the suspects in handcuffs on the ground – and to the cops in uniform around the house.

Less than a mile from the monastery's front yard is the Mississippi River, and some of the most peaceful times in my life have been walking with the Sisters downstream, with the Minneapolis downtown skyline ahead of us.

Mary Frances and I like to have an early supper at Broadway Pizza and walk the bank on a summer evening before the sun goes down. We have each scattered the ashes of a loved one in the water. We have watched kayakers, water skiers, and fishermen navigating the tricky currents. We have shooed the Canada geese from our path. But mostly, we have walked in silence, aware of the power and peace of moving water. I am aware that the peace I feel walking along the banks of the Mississippi, the Father of Waters, is inextricably intertwined with my journey with the Sisters.

"When I find myself in times of trouble, Mother Mary comes to me, speaking words of wisdom: Let It Be."
                                                            – The Beatles

Way Beyond 12 Steps

When I was asked by Sister Mary Margaret McKenzie to join a 12-Step group to deal with the corrosive effects of white privilege on her life and others, I was skeptical. I've been going to 12-Step meetings for more than 15 years and I couldn't quite see how this would work.

Such a group could turn into a debating society—edgy, angry and defensive. I thought AA's goal was simple: to help people abstain from drugs and alcohol. But the more I thought about it, those 12 steps are a blueprint to living a spiritual life of honesty, humility, integrity, and charity. And that's what Mary Margaret's life, and those of her six Visitation Sisters, has been about—for almost thirty years in north Minneapolis.

But this was Mary Margaret doing the asking, and she's been an elder, a mentor, an adviser, and a spiritual mother to me since we first met in 1989. When I'm down on one knee sucking for air, I run to Margaret for comfort and counsel.

I also think Mary Margaret, still dealing with the effects of a stroke she suffered in 2016, has a desire to put her spiritual house in good order. Part of that process would entail dealing with circumstances that shaped her life: one of which was growing up white in Decatur, Illinois, and going to college at Marquette in Milwaukee, Wisconsin.

I haven't thought much about white privilege, but I grew up in Fond du Lac, sixty miles north of Milwaukee. As I reflect on it, I had all the advantages: a stable home, a steady income, a good school, a welcoming community—and a grandmother with some money to take us traveling to California. So maybe I was a part of what Margaret sought to examine.

She chose the first participants in this group of ten that meets once a month on a Sunday afternoon. We are black and white, men and women, younger and older. We are bound by a desire to heal old wounds, make amends, and improve our awareness of the plights and problems of our brothers and sisters.

Like our AA predecessors, we listen as much as we talk. What is said in the meeting stays in the meeting. Our desire is not to "fix" our colleagues but to heal ourselves—by talking honestly, listening carefully, and thinking soulfully.

The steps we follow are lifted out of the AA Big Book, something we do with respect and reverence. We have tailored them carefully to suit our mission.

It begins with the first step:

"Admitted we were powerless over the pervasive and persistent presence of white privilege and its resulting racism and bigotry and that our lives have become less than they could be." It's followed by the second: "Came to believe that a power greater than ourselves could restore us to the loving, caring human beings we are intended to be."

The last step, twelve, comes directly from AA's Big Book, with no change at all: "Having had a spiritual awakening as a result of these steps, we tried to carry this message to others and to practice these principles in all our affairs."

Our first meeting was in January, 2018, and we've shared stories that are poignant and powerful. Mary Margaret set the tone in that initial meeting when she read from a poem by Maya Angelou, "Touched by an Angel":

To liberate us into life.
Love arrives
And in its train come ecstasies
Old memories of pleasure
Ancient histories of pain.
Yet if we are bold
Love strikes away the chains of fear
From our souls.

To one degree or another, our souls are laid bare in these meetings, sometimes with resentments about the discrimination of police officers, Christian clergy, and public officials. And sometimes it's the residual guilt from our own good fortune.

I recall an incident when I was a high school senior, riding around on a Friday night with a couple of guys I didn't know very well. We pulled into a gas station, bought a couple of bucks' worth and, before we left, one of the guys lifted a tin of car wax and slipped it into his back pocket. I didn't know about it until we were a mile away, but then again, I didn't insist that we go back and return it.

The next day a police officer appeared at my door. The station owner had "made" one of the guys from a photo in a high school year book and he, in turn, fingered me as a ride-along. I quickly "fessed up" and the cop gave me a five-minute lecture on the doorstep about honor and honesty. He also told my father. What he did NOT do was arrest me.

I have no doubt had I been a black kid, he'd have taken me downtown, written me up, and saddled me with a record. I got away clean and that's the way I entered the U.S. Army and the University of Wisconsin. That seems to me to describe white privilege.

I've heard enough stories from the black men at our meeting to know they were not afforded the same privilege I got from a cop who knew my father. In fact, one of them had a story with an ending 180 degrees from my get-off-free experience. He was out with his wife early on a Saturday morning in a north Minneapolis suburb, driving to Cub on Broadway, where they liked to shop when the store was empty.

On the way they spotted a group of four squad cars in a parking lot. He slowed down to see what was going on and rolled to a stop. Within a minute a squad was in back of him with red lights flashing. He rolled down the window, the cop came over and asked to see his driver's license, proof of insurance, and auto registration.

License: Valid. Insurance: In Force. Registration: To His Name.

"What'd I do?" he asked.

"You came to a rolling stop at the sign," the cop said. Then he asked him to step out of the car.

"Have you been drinking?" the cop asked.

"I had two glasses of wine," he said, "kind of celebrating with my wife for paying off some old debts." Those two glasses merited a field sobriety test. Finger to your nose. Count backwards from 25. Stand on one foot. He said he did all of them without a hitch.

Then he said Yes to a breathalyzer test and blew a .11, three one-hundredths over the .08 threshold. The cop cuffed him, had his car towed, and told his wife to walk home. He admitted he cried in the back seat of the squad, asking for a break—afraid he might lose his job.

No way. He was booked, fingerprinted, and allowed to leave jail, less than an hour and a half after he was arrested. Apparently police didn't think he was too inebriated to hit the streets. I believe he was stopped that night for being black, being on the street after midnight, and being inquisitive about what the squads were doing in the parking lot.

He told the story at one of our group meetings. When I was a younger guy, I would have listened, told him how sorry I was, and gone on with my agenda, my business, my career. Now I have no career but I do have time and maybe an eye for redemption. So I called an old lawyer friend who knew the best DWI attorney in Hennepin County. We persuaded him to discount his fee and managed to raise the rest.

In less than two months, the lawyer got the case reviewed, the charge reduced, and the license restored. In effect, he saved his client's job, kept him and his family whole. He was amazed at how quick it moved, how easy it appeared, how slick it seemed. The irony was not lost on him.

"NO way I could have found or afforded this guy," he said later. "This is not the kind of lawyer most of the 'brothers' get to work for them. Yep, no way that's usual." The whole deal was anything but usual: The victim of white privilege became its beneficiary. And I got a chance to put my money where my mouth is.

When we started our little group, I wondered how steps promulgated to deal with an addiction would relate to an attitude. Months later, I'm satisfied the answer is—they work. We belong in this milieu. And I've learned a little more about myself. I should be more grateful for what I've got. I had a lot of help along the way and hardly a handicap. Oh, as a teenager I thought being short (5'6") was a real disadvantage.

Compared to growing up in Clarksdale, Mississippi, without a father, a house, or a playground, I had it made. This 12-step program, however it's applied, can keep me grateful; it also requires me to be useful, helpful. It's right in the last paragraph of the first half of AA's Big Book:

"Abandon yourself to God as you understand God. Admit your faults to God and to your fellows. Clear away the wreckage of your past. Give freely of what you find and join us. We shall be with you in the fellowship of the spirit and you will surely meet some of us as you trudge the Road of Happy Destiny."

Thanks to Mary Margaret, that road just got a little wider.

The Lion in Winter

My first recollection of Jim Klobuchar was in the winter of 1965-66 when I was a young police reporter for the *Minneapolis Star*, fresh from the School of Journalism at the University of Wisconsin. Klobuchar had just come to the *Star* from the Minneapolis Tribune, where he'd been a sports writer after leaving a similar post at the Associated Press.

His stories about the Minnesota Vikings and encounters with Coach Norm Van Brocklin were almost legendary. In my opinion he was, quite simply, the best newspaper writer in the Twin Cities. He could turn a phrase, spin a yarn, afflict the comfortable and comfort the afflicted. His reporting and writing reflected a newspaper man who was peerless and fearless.

I'd never seen him up close until a stormy day that winter, with more than a foot and a half of snow on the ground. I'd been living on Powderhorn Terrace in south Minneapolis, and that morning I walked to work down the middle of Park Avenue because my car was plowed in; the managing editor came to work on a snowmobile.

I was congratulating myself as I walked in the front door of the building at 425 Portland Avenue at 7 a.m., figuring I would be one of the first in the newsroom. Klobuchar was already sitting at the city desk, a pair of head phones over his ears. He was talking to a highway patrolman on the Iron Range about road conditions. He had already finished one storm roundup story and was working on his second, about travel conditions around the state. Before the morning was over, he'd write a third—a feature about a young family that was stranded by the storm and had to be rescued.

He was a journalistic whirling dervish: fast, confidant, thorough, and graceful. Over the next dozen years, Jim and I developed a friendship centered around work. I followed his column and his exploits: climbing mountain tops, hiking forest trails, biking across the state, holding football clinics, and searching for Sasquatch. He was in constant motion and I often wondered how he did it. What I didn't wonder about is the price he paid.

He was getting divorced from his first wife, Rose, the mother of his daughters. Years later, he very publicly admitted it was painful for him and the girls. He was also drinking excessively, something that would plague him for another two decades. While Jim's personal demons escaped my attention, his professional eccentricities did not—especially when I became the *Star*'s managing editor. That meant the kid from Wisconsin was now Jim's boss.

Jim, it seemed to me, was a guy who felt his cup was never quite full. He was always thirsty. He wanted to write more, not less. He wanted a bigger role, not smaller. He wanted to be front and center, never back and to the side. He was more attuned to demands and deadlines than comfort and contemplation. When a big story broke, he wanted a part of it. He was a newsroom star and he wanted to be treated that way,

For the most part that wasn't a problem. Occasionally it was, like the time I asked Jim—delicately, I thought—to consider writing fewer columns each week so he could spend more time on the ones he did write. "You deserve a more leisurely pace," I intoned, "one that'll give you more time for reporting and reflection." He bristled and got ready for a fight.

I backtracked and took a fade. It wasn't worth the pain.

It was a different story, however, when Jim was consistently late in meeting the copy deadline with his column. That meant it was late to the copy desk, the composing room and, finally, to the press itself. Not making home deliveries on time was a circulation nightmare and I had talked to Jim about the problem. He'd nod, talk about needing the deadline pressure to write, and vow do better in the future. That future came on a Tuesday morning when the column was late to the composing room and I ordered the paper to go to press WITHOUT the Klobuchar column on the cover page of the metro section.

I went to my office and prepared for the assault. It turned out to be more of an encounter. Jim said he was disappointed in me, choosing to enforce a "chickenshit" rule at the expense of the Star's readers. I told him he was entitled to his opinion but I thought I was just doing my job. He huffed out, and I sat for a few minutes, and then felt a sudden urge to hit the men's room. On the way I happened to look out the third-floor window.

Klobuchar was across the street. I watched him kick over the newspaper box in front of the Associated Press office. He turned away and then came back and put the box upright. I wondered whether I had just kicked away the paper's franchise. I did not. The next day, Jim was at his desk writing his column, which hit the copy desk fifteen minutes before the deadline.

I was well into the third year of my reign as Jim's boss when Steve Isaacs, newly arrived from the *Washington Post*, became my boss. He thought of the *Star* as too traditional, conventional, and predictable. He wanted an evening newspaper that "glowed in the dark." I wasn't sure what that meant. I was sure it was time to leave. Klobuchar and Barbara Flanagan took me out to lunch at Mayslack's on my last day. The day after, Jim wrote a column about my departure:

> *For those of you who haven't met him, I'd like to introduce Dave Nimmer on the occasion of his departure.*
>
> *He called the city room clan together a couple of days ago to announce his resignation as managing editor of the* Minneapolis Star. *Years ago, Dave Nimmer envisioned himself in the role of a brick-tough managing editor, with his sleeves rolled up and coarse and probably pungent directives rolling off his tongue an hour before deadline. It was a portrait that required some resourcefulness because Davey has the general dimensions of an apprentice jockey, and too much whim and forgiveness in his innards to make a credible tyrant.*
>
> *He did make a remarkably good managing editor for a man who is fundamentally a reporter, tuned to all of the 'electricities' and scents that animate a good reporter—and in Dave's case, a great reporter.*

They gave me a boat and trailer when I left the paper, but the best gift was Jim's column, which catalogued my editor's career with incredible grace and generosity. I sent it to my dad because Jim had described what I wanted to be, and what I was, better than I could have. After I got to WCCO Television as a reporter, and eventually to the University of St. Thomas, I continued to read Klobuchar's column, until he retired in 1995. He always spoke my language: supporter of underdogs, tormentor of phonies, and deflator of airbags. He wrote with sympathy and sensitivity of the human condition and its frailties.

His own were sometimes very public, including several

arrests for drunken driving and a suspension for making up a quote in one of his columns. I thought about reaching out to him but didn't. Jim would occasionally put words in the mouths of good sources, who never objected. I always suspected they thought Klobuchar wrote it better than they could have said it.

I saw Jim in person at a retirement fête at the University of Minnesota. I was invited to speak briefly by his daughter, Amy. I sat on the stage next to Judge Miles Lord, who was a helluva lot edgier and funnier than I was. Miles and Jim shared that Iron Range humor—real, raucous, and rarely restrained.

I rarely saw Jim until a few months after his eighty-eighth birthday celebration, which I missed because I was out of town. Norton Stillman, an iconic figure in the Twin Cities' book community who had published several of Jim's books, called me a couple of months later and suggested we have lunch with him. So Norton, whose press had also published my book of short stories, and I picked Jim up at his St. Louis Park apartment and drove to a nearby Chinese restaurant

Jim looked thinner. He walked slower. He talked softer. He seemed smaller. But, dammit, he was still Klobuchar and it was good to see him. The next time I saw him was at a seniors' residence in Wayzata, and I brought along Jim Shoop and Bob Hentges, two of his former *Star* colleagues. With one number or another, we followed Jim to a nursing and "memory care" center in Edina, aware of the irony that the man who poked so much fun at the Edina "cake eaters" was now living in their backyard.

The old newspaperman was slowly fading away. The essence of the man was not, however, and it shined brightly whenever he greeted us for our monthly lunches. A smile would crease his face. And he always said the same thing:

"Boys, it's so good to see you." Then we'd tell stories, talk politics, and share moments. "Remember," Jim said, "when the city editor would stand up and shout 'Any late ones?'" That would be late stories, and Lee Canning did the shouting.

From lunch to lunch, the mood was light hearted. But each time Jim ate less. The pauses were longer, the gaps wider. But our connection grew stronger. Toward the end of one of the lunches I sensed a moment, an opportunity that one ought to seize. Jim and I were sitting next to each other. The conversation had dwindled; the room was quiet. I leaned forward, putting my hand on his wrist. "Jim," I said, "how are you? How are you?" He looked neither surprised nor offended by the question. It seemed like a minute passed before he spoke.

When he did, he leaned even closer to me. "Davey," he replied, "mostly, I'm grateful." I waited for more but he spoke no more. The man who must have written six or seven million words in his newspaper life answered my question in three.

A Second Chance

I got the phone call from Kris on Saturday before Labor Day, 2013, just after I got back from a Canadian fishing trip. Though we'd been divorced for eight years, we kept in touch, honoring the 18 years we spent together and the love we had shared. During the last years of our marriage, we had set out on very different spiritual paths, and though I didn't think it mattered that much, it made Kris feel that we were heading in quite different directions. I accepted that, and we moved on from our farmhouse in Afton to new and separate lives. After developing a little scar tissue, we both found it easy to stay in touch.

Kris asked how I was doing, and I told her the crown on one of my teeth had split in half that morning as I ate my breakfast cereal. "I've had better days," I said.

"So have I," she said. And she told me she'd collapsed while walking around Lake of the Isles with a friend earlier in the day. Doctors in the emergency room couldn't figure out why one of her legs went numb, and she was going to get a more thorough exam the following week.

I told her everything would turn out okay, and asked her to call me when she knew more. What I didn't say was I thought it might be a complication from the lymphoma (Waldenstrom's) she'd been treated for a couple of years before. It was in remission but Kris continued to struggle with side effects of the chemotherapy.

I next heard from her three weeks later as she was about to have surgery on a disc that doctors thought might be impinging on a nerve, causing her leg to give way. I saw her the day before surgery, and again a few hours after it was done. The procedure was relatively minor but she'd need to go to a rehabilitation home for a few days since she lived alone in a two-story house.

I decided to accompany her to the rehab place that evening and thus began a four-month odyssey that was the most painful and poignant, gritty and graceful, in my life. Nothing I've done before or since has come close.

One of the most graceful acts came from my friend and companion, Cindy Lamont, who told me to do whatever I needed with, and for, Kris. I did my best to keep her abreast of where I was going, how I was doing, and what was happening.

The first rehab stop after surgery went well for Kris. She was released after five days; she'd climbed up stairs, walked down hallways, and gotten up from the toilet. In the meantime, I'd established a pattern of watering her plants, feeding the stray cats that appeared on her porch, and making sure that the lights were off and the doors were locked before I left.

When she got back home, Kris found the place in good shape and, for almost a month, she watered her own plants, cooked her meals, and fed the neighborhood kitties. In between, I took her to half a dozen visits for physical therapy, CAT scans, and MRI tests. Her legs were not getting any stronger and she'd fallen twice. Each time I brought her home, it was a little harder for her and sadder for me. It was tough to watch this vital and vigorous woman struggle to walk the path from the garage to the back porch and to climb the stairs.

She was convinced the problem was with her spine: deteriorating discs, pinched nerves, misaligned vertebrae.

Her friends and I thought she'd needed a complete physical workup but she said the x-rays indicated her "back was a mess" and spinal fusion surgery was the answer. Kris was always quick to make up her mind, to develop a plan, and to get on with it. And she did, without pausing for a second opinion. A respected orthopedic surgeon with an impressive record scheduled the surgery for November 1, and Kris asked me to accompany her to the hospital.

By this time, she needed a Medivan (and a wheelchair) and we both arrived at her house at 9 a.m. on a sunny Friday morning. She was teary as the attendant loaded her into the van. She looked small and lonely, sitting in the wheelchair in the back of the van. "I wish you could ride with me," she said.

"I'll follow you," I replied, and we met at the intake desk at St. John's Hospital in Maplewood.

An hour later, she was on a gurney in a white-walled surgery prep room, wearing a hospital gown, with an IV in her arm and a heart monitor on her chest. The surgeon came in and matter-of-factly described the procedure, which included rearranging her abdominal organs, exposing the spinal column and then putting her back together. I couldn't look at Kris. I had trouble dealing with the trepidation in my head.

I held her hand as the orderlies wheeled her down the hall to the operating room. She looked at me, squeezed my hand, and said softly, "David, you do know that love is the only thing that matters." With that, she was gone. I saw her the next day, the most painful after surgery. She was heavily sedated but the discomfort didn't let go. I sat next to her bed, with my head on her leg and my hand clutching hers. We stayed that way for more than an hour.

The pain subsided after two days and Kris was moved to a rehabilitation center at the Masonic Home in Bloomington.

She'd be there for almost two months, and during that time she was never able to stand on her own.

For the first few weeks she made some progress, and friends showed up with a special blanket, gourmet snacks, and an I-Pad. She liked her therapists and tried her best to move her legs and tone her body, which was encased in a plastic cast from her shoulders to her waist. It looked decidedly uncomfortable but she persevered.

I spent Thanksgiving with Cindy while Kris's friends brought the turkey, dressing, sweet potatoes, and cranberry sauce to her. She said she had a good day and I thought maybe she was on the cusp of a recovery. However, a few days later the staff noticed that one side of her face was drooping and decided she might have suffered a stroke.

As I came to the home for a routine visit on Friday afternoon, Kris was being wheeled out to an ambulance, headed for St. John's Hospital. I tried to follow in rush-hour traffic but it took me an hour and a half to get from Bloomington to Maplewood. When I got to the hospital, Kris was in the emergency room, in another white-walled cubicle with various machines, meters and monitors to provide a speedy diagnosis.

For Kris, the consensus was she probably did not have a stroke, but doctors needed an MRI to be sure. And it would be several hours before the magnetic tube was available. I realized we hadn't eaten and I asked Kris whether she'd like a sandwich. She said she would. "I'll get you one from the cafeteria," I said.

"Aren't you having one?" she asked. No, I told her, I thought I'd go home to catch *Blue Bloods*, the police drama we both liked.

Kris, who was lying on an exam table, motioned for me to get up from my chair and come over. She grabbed my hand. "Eat with me," she said. "I'm so tired of being alone." I got two sandwiches and two bottles of water. I sat next to her with a sandwich in one hand and her hand in the other.

I left St. John's about 10 p.m., just before she got the MRI. She called around midnight and said the test revealed no stroke and an ambulance took her back to the Masonic Home, where she stayed for two more weeks before the staff determined she was no longer a rehab candidate. At that point she moved to an assisted living facility on Ford Parkway in St. Paul.

It quickly became apparent she needed round-the-clock help—to eat, bathe, and even sit. Her primary care doctor admitted Kris to St. Joseph's Hospital on January 14, believing her condition was rapidly deteriorating. She was right. In the first week at St. Joe's, Kris ate little, slept a lot, and when awake was mostly agitated, anxious, and angry. "Get me out of here, David," she'd say. "Please take me home." I'd tell her I couldn't do that and she'd sigh and look at me with her sad eyes.

The one bright moment I observed was when a coworker from the Pollution Control Agency came all the way down from Brainerd to see Kris. I listened as the young woman told her that she'd been a great teacher, mentor, and friend. "You gave me courage," she said, "and showed me how to handle those big shots who liked to talk loud and threaten."

That fit the Kris I knew. As a lawyer in private practice before she joined the PCA, Kris managed real estate deals and was used to dealing with "suits," fearless in the face of bluster and bravado that often accompanied the negotiations.

By the second week at St. Joe's, Kris was slipping in and out of consciousness. She wasn't eating. She wasn't talking. She was sipping a little water every couple of hours. Her doctors never said she was dying but when I asked one whether that wasn't what was happening, he seemed relieved.

"Oh, yes," he said, "perhaps you should talk with the hospice people." Kris's executor and long-time faithful friend, Robin Keyworth, and I did that and thus began the final days. On one of them, Kris's oncologist talked with us and we all agreed we should tell Kris the reality of her condition. And we did—on a Thursday afternoon as the sun set.

"Kris," the oncologist said, "we are out of options. Your Waldenstrom's lymphoma is back and you're too weak to withstand a rigorous chemo regimen, with all of the side effects, and your hair falling out."

I'll never forget what Kris said, in a clear, crisp voice. "I don't care about my hair," she replied. Those were the last words I ever heard from her. They were a true indication of how much she wanted to live.

Robin, her husband, Steve, and I sat with Kris pretty much throughout the weekend, taking turns holding her hand, wiping her brow, telling our stories. Mostly, she seemed peaceful, although at times she'd twitch and turn, and nothing I did seemed to offer comfort. It was, and always had been, out of my control.

I left the hospital on Sunday afternoon, wondering how long it would be and why she couldn't die while we were at her side. That evening, before I went to bed, I received an e-mail from the Visitation Monastery of Minneapolis, the five Sisters who knew both of us well and had held my hand through the divorce.

For most of the eighteen Christmases Kris and I were together, we had spent part of Christmas Eve with the Sisters in North Minneapolis. Sometimes we had dinner with them and sometimes we only exchanged greetings and a prayer. They were part of our lives.

The e-mail from Mary Frances Reis was like a last rite,

one which she asked me to read to Kris on behalf of the community. They said they loved her, they prayed for her, and bid goodbye to her. They included a short prayer from Therese of Lisieux. Kris and I had been to the Basilica of Lisieux, and I recall her telling me she felt she had known the saint—The Little Flower—in a past life.

" Kris," the Sisters wrote, "may your precious St. Therese of Lisieux companion you on your final journey to the full embrace of Spirit. Into Spirit's hands we commend yours." I received the e-mail at 10:15 p.m.

Shortly thereafter, I got a call from Robin. She said the hospital had just called. Kris died at 10:20 p..m.—January 26, 2014.

Letters I Never Wrote

The return address was unfamiliar but it was handwritten and so was my name and address. I was not the "occupant," nor was I being solicited for a contribution that would be matched three-for-one by an anonymous donor.

I opened the envelop and took out a one-page letter, also handwritten:

Nim,

> *I hope this letter finds you well. I'm writing to simply say Thank You. It has been 25 years since I had the privilege of being a pure pain in the ass for you. I remember challenging many of the assertions you offered and thinking I had all the answers. Your patience, insight, commitment and storytelling changed my world. I learned to apply a journalistic filter to every issue."*

My first thought was "Are you sure it's me you're thinking of?" But I remembered Terri Moore (then Teuber), and she was careful and skeptical. She also had plenty of experience: ten years as a TV reporter, ten years as communication director for the Nebraska governor, U.S. Senator, and Secretary of Agriculture, and two years in the White House as a deputy press secretary for policy and planning. What the hell, I took the compliment and returned it with equal sincerity and clarity—in a handwritten letter.

I wrote that the Hastings native was not only NOT a

pain in the ass, but she was an asset in the classroom at the University of St. Thomas. She read the textbook, kept up with the news, and came to the class with informed ideas. She was, in fact, a teacher's best friend.

In addition to my letter, Terri sent forty-nine others. "I'm turning 50 this year, " she wrote, "and decided to write letters to 50 people to mark the occasion." What a generous, gracious thing to do—something I've never done and never thought

Terri Moore

about until I read her letter. I certainly have been, for a good part of my life, self-important, self-involved, and self-centered. I don't view it as an indictment, but more like a passage to a more enlightened time.

And at this time I can't think of fifty people to write to, but I can think of eight, one for every decade. They are teachers, mentors, and sponsors; most of them are dead, and a few relatively unknown and unappreciated.

I met the first one in eighth grade at Roosevelt Junior High School in Fond du Lac, Wis. She was **Grace Hemble**, who taught an English class. She was a funny, feisty, and sprightly teacher, who taught me to diagram sentences, read the Pogo comic strip, and write a simple essay. She was the first to tell me I was a good writer and I remember how empowering that felt.

While Ms. Hemble was important to me, I believe she was largely ignored by school administrators. I could not find her name in a Google search, and she always seemed to be alone in the hallways. She was a rebel who lived in an uptight town, a spinster who took care of an ailing mother and smoked Camel cigarettes. That didn't make her mainstream in 1954 but it sure made her memorable—to me.

The similarities between her and another memorable teacher, **Marie Stepnoski,** are remarkable. Both were single women caring for ailing mothers. Both taught English and were energetic and demanding in their classrooms. Stepnoski ("Step," behind her back) was my teacher as a senior at Goodrich High School. She introduced us to Shakespeare, T. S. Elliot, and Samuel Coleridge and "The Rhyme of the Ancient Mariner." She had us read aloud from the poets' works and I discovered I could be a pretty fair actor and a damned good reader.

Step also taught me the finer points of writing: the active voice, strong verbs, short sentences, and parallel construction. She taught me to lift my prose, as I delicately put it, "out of the loon shit and into the clear blue sky."

It strikes me now that both women would have appreciated a note of gratitude from me. Neither made much money, garnered public attention, or got special accolades. They simply taught kids with raging hormones to read and write with a reverence that gave me a gift I didn't know I had.

On the other hand, **Professor William Hachten,** from the University of Wisconsin's School of Journalism, was well paid, widely recognized, and highly regarded. When I met him in my first class at UW, Beginning News Writing, he was the department's newest faculty member. He had a degree from Stanford University, a Ph. D. from the University of Minnesota, several years of experience with California dailies, and one year of professional football with the New York Giants.

My resume was not quite as impressive. When I sat

down at my desk, I noticed a typewriter. I didn't know how to type. Professor Hachten gently explained I'd have to learn, and he assured me I would be able to hunt-and-peck with a couple hours' practice. Within a week I was typing as fast as I could form a coherent sentence. First came the lede—the news burst—then the supporting facts and, finally, a concluding paragraph.

The first real news story I wrote in class was about the death of gangster John Dillinger, in a shootout with the FBI in front of Chicago's Biograph Theater. Hachten noted my lede was "newsy," my facts correct, and my grammar acceptable. However, he allowed as how the story was "jumpy," lacking transitions from paragraph to paragraph. I think I got a B; the professor was a compassionate man.

He not only taught me the basics of news writing, he engineered a trip to a national journalism convention in Miami Beach, where I met David Brinkley. Hachten told me I was good enough to work for a metro daily, and went so far as to set up an interview with a recruiter for the *Minneapolis Star and Tribune*. I suspect he relied on his heart, not his head; he was smart enough to become a respected scholar on the press in developing African countries. That interview led to my first job out of college, after only three months of actual reporting experience with my hometown daily.

While Bill Hachten helped me with the practical part of my college education, **Professor A. Campbell Garnett** added to its philosophical and spiritual depth. His course on Religion and the Moral Life came in my senior year as my mother was dying of ovarian cancer. I was pretty much done with God and organized religion, and those believers who said prayers would save her. They prayed. I prayed. She died.

Professor Garnett offered the notion that a man of reason

147

could believe in a God of love. He appeared as gentle and gracious as his philosophy: He was slight and short, with white hair and fingers gnarled by arthritis. He turned pages in a text with the heel of his hand. During the spring semester, he frequently held classes on a hillside overlooking Lake Mendota.

He argued that we experience God from within, a kind of innate sense we have of right and wrong, that transcends cultural norms and government laws. God, he said, is omniscient, not omnipotent. Garnett's God did not decide who was on the 35W Bridge the day it collapsed, nor did he, or *could* she, interfere in the daily flow of life. This was a loving God, but not all powerful, not able to stop the Holocaust or kill the cancer. It helped me to accept my mother's plight, and I carried his "simple theism" with me for sixty years.

When I moved from the classroom in Madison to the newsroom in Minneapolis, the *Star*'s city editor, **Lee Canning,** was more interested in my adaptability than my spirituality, my tenacity than my theology. I had one suit, two white shirts, two ties, a crew cut, and horn-rimmed glasses. I looked like a high school freshman trying to find his homeroom.

On my third morning in the newsroom, one of the veteran reporters pulled a sheet of copy paper from her typewriter and looked at me. "Hey boy," she said, "take this to the city desk." I grabbed it and dropped it in front of Canning. He looked at me quizzically. He asked me why I did this. I told him the woman seated three rows away told me to do it. Canning grabbed my suit cuff.

He dragged me over to her desk. "Bev," he said, "believe it or not, this is a goddamn new reporter, not a copy boy. So please, not again." She was embarrassed. I was mortified. Canning was unaffected. From that day on, he chose to regard me as a real reporter, not a raw rookie. He gave me the cop beat, picked me to cover city hall, and made me an investigative reporter. Finally, he appointed me managing editor of the paper at the age of thirty-four. The truth is I always viewed him as more of a father figure than an editor.

Floyd O. also filled the role of father/mentor in my life. I met him in a meeting of the River Rats, a group that gathered weekly in a church in Afton. He'd been going to meetings like that for almost fifty years. I thought of him as a wise man— gentle, loving, and forgiving. What impressed me was: here is this wise man, his life seemingly serene and together, always working on himself, getting rid of bad habits and glomming on to new ideas.

I recall having coffee one morning with Floyd in the library at the University of St. Thomas. We were sitting at a table surrounded by a bunch of students, most of whom were not talking but intently staring at the screens on their smart phones. I was whining to Floyd about getting older, losing friends, and forgetting names. He smiled and then put his hand on my wrist. "Nim," he said, "in this life pain is inevitable. BUT MISERY, MY BOY, IS OPTIONAL." It was just the gentle kick in the ass I needed and, to my credit, I felt it and moved it from my butt to my heart.

I never did tell Floyd how helpful he'd been, nor did I write to him before he died. But the last two letters on my list are to people still alive, none more so than **Steven Lybrand,** who I believe is a hotshot jury consultant on the West Coast. When I knew him he was a sociology professor at the University of St. Thomas, and he was THE faculty member who made me feel most welcome when I came to the university from the WCCO Newsroom.

I had a lowly B.S. degree among the cluster of Ph.D.'s. I suspected some of my colleagues thought of me as an ink-stained wretch, who came over to teach the inverted pyramid to job-seeking journalists. Lybrand, with his Ph.D from the University of Wisconsin, gave me the benefit of the doubt from our first meeting.

The two of us put together a documentary about the effects of poverty on families in the Twin Cities and Wisconsin. We tried to show what happens when work is hard to find, a home is hard to rent, and the future is hard to see. Lybrand supplied the theories and themes and I brought them to life with pictures, words, and talking heads. The doc ran in prime time on Twin Cities Public Television, and we showed it again at the annual meeting of the American Sociological Association in Chicago. Steven was a mentor who helped me find safe passage through the halls of academe.

He also taught me something about putting your money where your mouth is. He gave assistance to the families we pictured in the documentary. He took kids to the clinic, bought baskets of groceries and helped families cut bureaucratic red tape. I knew I had to fall in line so, together, Steven and I helped a former gangster get a car, brought some used furniture to a single dad, and found a job at St. Thomas for a welfare mother. The lesson from Lybrand was simple: sometimes you ought to be more than a reporter. You might want to think about being a helper.

Professor Lybrand steered me toward a niche on a university campus. **The River Rats** helped me find comfort in the human condition. This group of twenty or so men and women, from thirty to eighty, have at one time or another been down on one knee sucking for air or staring in a mirror wondering what happened to the person they used to be.

One step at a time, they have been walking with me on a path toward courage and compassion, honesty and humility, serenity and service. If this sounds like a Sermon on the Mount prescription, it's not. For me, it's simply basic training for what a good man is—and what he does. My River Rats lay it out with a sense of humor. When I was sharing my struggle with self-centeredness, one old-timer smiled. "Yep," he said, "like you, I'm really not anybody important anymore. But I'm all I think about all day long."

What I'm thinking about now is the irony: a former student giving her teacher the last and most important lesson. All that's left for an old man to do is put it in writing and mail a letter.

The Last Hand at Pickerel Arm

The passage of time and the vagaries of age are never more obvious than at Pickerel Arm of Minnitaki Lake, 150 miles north of International Falls into Ontario. When we first began going to the fishing camp, eight of us stood for a picture on the deck of the cabin we'd rented. I came back this year at the age of 79, with Ron Handberg, 81, and Jim Shoop, now 87. We are officially the survivors. I've attended the funerals for all five of our departed brothers: Ted, Tom, Andy, Lub, and The Bear.

This figures to be our last trip, although we've been saying that for the past few years. But it's also true that the character of the annual trip has changed considerably. Lub, my friend from high school, used to buy the groceries at the commissary of the U.S. airbase in Altus, Oklahoma. He was meticulous in his accounting, figuring out the cost-per-ounce and recording the item's price for all to see.

This year Jim and I bought the same stuff at Cub and recorded no prices. We finished shopping in forty-five minutes, with Jim grumbling that I "was running through the store," with little regard for price or quality.

The 475-mile drive from the Twin Cities to the camp now takes about ten hours; we used to do it in eight. We leave earlier because we have to stop more: We stretch. We pee. About every hundred miles or two hours, whichever comes first. Then, we eat.

The original group

We're more apt to choose fast food or franchise fare. The old restaurants, like Rudy's at Cloquet, are long gone. The Egg McMuffin has replaced scrambled eggs with hash browns, bacon, and toast.

When we get to the border at International Falls, we still have 150 miles and about four hours to go. It used to be the border crossing was perfunctory, though slightly funnier coming from Canada into the U.S.:

Border agent: Did you buy anything? No.

Agent: Did you catch anything? Yes.

Agent: Did you shoot anything? No (laughing)

It got a little more complicated after 9/11. Now we need a passport. We need to look serious. We need to roll down all the windows. And we need to answer more questions: Where are you from? Where are you going? How long are you staying? Do you have any firearms? Do you have any live bait?

For the three of us, the whole process still moves rather quickly. The agents probably aren't on the lookout for any terrorists in their eighties. Once across the border, our next stop is Dryden, a mill town with an airport, a hospital, a Walmart, and a Safeway grocery store where we buy the perishables.

When we were eight, Lub led the shopping brigade; we followed dutifully and chose as he directed. The grocery cart was a cholesterol catastrophe, loaded with brats, bacon, eggs, and cheese. Now, the three of us shopped without a clear chain of command, and the collaboration resulted in more cereal, fruit, and fiber. We did buy a package of Johnsonville brats in deference to Lub.

What we didn't buy—a must in the past—was beer and liquor: at least two cases of Labatt's Blue and at least one bottle of Scotch and one of Crown Royal. This year we came into Canada with two twelve-packs of diet soda. Ron did have a pint of brandy which lasted for the week. Years ago that would have been the first twenty minutes of Happy Hour.

Our first day fishing in Pickerel Arm was not particularly happy. It was more a test of recall, strength, timing, and unity. It was not easy to relocate that cobblestone shoreline where we caught the walleyes in 2015. It was hard to control the boat when back-trolling into a stiff wind, with a rod in one hand and the other on the tiller of a 50-horsepower Yamaha. With my short arms, I was bent at a 45-degree angle to get my line in the water.

For almost three hours, I was taking spray in the face and cold water on my crotch. And having gripped the motor handle tightly to control the boat for most of that time, I had to peel the fingers back from the claw that my left hand had become when we got back to the cabin.

Bites came hard that first day, and we all missed fish because we weren't sure how long to wait before setting the hook. We wisely did know enough to stick together and keep our mouths shut when we encountered trouble—through no

The last three compatriots—Jim, Nim, and Ron

fault of our own, of course. Trying to jerk his trolling rig loose from a rock, Jim forgot to keep his thumb on the reel spool and wound up with a backlash as big as a robin's nest. Neither Ron nor I said a word. We did not laugh. We did not smile. We tried to look serious and sympathetic.

When we got back to the dock, we had two walleyes to show for a day's fishing. On the plus side, no one drowned. I didn't run the boat ashore. We found our way back. And the pound of leeches we bought was probably going to last us for the entire week.

The next four days were more like old times, with a few obvious acknowledgments to time and technology. The wind died down. The sun came out. It got easier to run the motor. The walleyes started to bite. Jim, the oldest, caught the most, but we each nailed a "trophy" fish.

We settled into the cabin routine that made up for what it lacked in spontaneity with sanity. Each morning we made the beds. We swept the floor, cooked the meals, and did the dishes. Unlike in the past, we actually had flat surfaces that were not covered with trinkets, tools, and tackle. We could walk across the floor without hearing a crunch. The walleyes tasted better at a dinner table in the cabin than on the lake at shore lunch; they were crisp and flaky, not burnt and greasy. We used to fry them in a half pound of Snowflake lard. You could almost hear your arteries harden.

What you couldn't hear in the old days was news of the outside world. This time we stayed in touch. Jim and I are technology averse and mask our fear with self-righteousness: let's not bastardize the wilderness solitude and serenity. Well, Ron brought his smart phone and laptop. Morning coffee, along with the early edition of the *Star Tribune*, never tasted better.

On the last day, as we packed our bags and paid the bill, we remembered the "staff" who had attended to our needs. That would be Sharon, a daily presence in a pair of tattered blue jeans. She dipped the minnows, cleaned the cabins, and filled the gas tanks—almost from dawn to dusk.

We used to leave a tip in an envelope with the camp owner. This year I wanted to say thank you and went to the room in the camp tool-and-ice house that she shares with her husband. Match stick-thin, Sharon has a weathered face and a practiced smile. "Thanks," I said, "for leaving our cabin so clean; the gleam from the inside of the refrigerator almost blinded us." She smiled and said she was just doing her job. You sure do it well. She smiled again. I could tell she was proud of her work and I walked back to the cabin believing those who serve us are no less worthy. She's working seventy hours while I'm having my hair cut, getting the car washed, shopping for groceries, and complaining about my busy week.

It felt good to know we were leaving her with a clean cabin—a tribute to my OCD—and we even scrubbed the stove top after finishing the supper dishes. We sat on the front porch facing the lake, which was mirror-like calm. The sun was slowly setting. The boats were lined up on the dock. The Canadian flag hung on a pole in the foreground. A pair of loons called to each other.

We talked of what a fine trip it had been, how much we enjoyed each other's company in spite of our jabs and gibes. I was a bit surprised that I wasn't sad. What I did feel was peaceful—and grateful. When the walleyes bit, the past disappeared and the present prevailed. We were forty years old again.

The Second Time Around

We had just rolled into Yellowstone National Park from Red Lodge, Montana, and I was tired from the previous day's drive. Cindy, who was born and raised in Wyoming, was excited to show me America's most famous chunk of real estate.

I was aware of her talking—to herself, too quiet for me to hear. "You know," I said, "you have a tendency to mumble, or I have a hearing problem." A pause.

"You do have a hearing problem," she replied.

"You don't have to shout," I said.

"I do," she said, "if I want you to hear me."

I spent the rest of the day somewhere between a sulk and a pout. By the next morning, however, we were having a pleasant breakfast overlooking Yellowstone Lake. We were back talking, walking, and smiling. The rest of the trip was a fine adventure, with hikes to backcountry lakes and a stay in Jackson Lake Lodge in the Grand Tetons.

The two-week road trip got me thinking that a "seniors" relationship does, indeed, require a pair of grownups. Lucinda Lamont and I had dated almost thirty years ago. Since then I had been married for eighteen years, divorced, and retired. Cindy had changed jobs, bought a house, and ended a relationship. So here we were, together again, with AARP cards instead of job titles.

And this stage in life, the boundaries are firmer, the habits stronger, and the edges sharper. What's harder is keeping the relationship centered firmly on that comfortable, compatible middle ground. With a few fits and starts, highs and lows, we've been able to do that and, in the process, put together a trusting, caring, and loving bulwark against the lightning bolts and paper cuts of growing older.

One of the strongest bonds is music, which is essential to both my life and in Cindy's. Music reaches a place in me that can unleash tears down my face or shivers up my spine. Cindy sings in the choir at St. Michael's Catholic Church in Stillwater. She's volunteered with the Minnesota Opera. She's stood in line at 7 a.m. on a chilly Saturday morning in April when tickets for Concerts at the Zoo go on sale at the Electric Fetus.

Together, we're trying it all, from blues to Beethoven, country to classics, from Northeast to Nashville. We're introducing each other to the music in our life. Cindy can sing a dozen Billy Joel songs from memory, hum a chorus from a Wagner opera, and "get down" with Florence and the Machine. And I, on the other hand, could take her to the Bluebird Café in Nashville.

The Bluebird is a kind of Holy Grail for country music, attracting songwriters who bring their guitars and sit in a group of four and sing each other's songs. The music is accompanied by good-natured banter and plays to an always appreciative audience of country fans who come to listen and not to talk.

I introduced Cindy to the Bluebird on a Wednesday night, and she was kind of surprised by how ordinary the place looked, sitting in a strip mall. We got there early, but soon the song writers began to gather – four of them. I didn't recognize any of the names, but they all chatted amiably and were pretty good guitar players. The least polished was the oldest: Wayland Holyfield.

When it came his turn, he smiled and told the crowd that when he was at a party and told folks he wrote songs for a living, the question was always the same: "So, tell me the name of a song you wrote?" Holyfield smiled and began to play. He was only a couple of bars into the song before I recognized "Could I Have This Dance for the Rest of My Life?" a hit for Anne Murray.

Pretty soon, I could hear Cindy singing softly along; then others joined in and I could hear some harmony: "When we're together it feels so right. Could I have this dance for the rest of my life?" Now we were both singing, and I couldn't recall when it felt so right—on a Wednesday night in a strip mall in Nashville.

On a Saturday afternoon at a Unitarian retreat center in the Arizona desert south of Tucson, Cindy repaid the favor. She found a gig by the Ronstadt Generations Band, having read a flyer tacked up on a bulletin board at a breakfast diner. She knew that the Ronstadts, including Linda, had been raised in Tucson. She put two and two together and said, "Let's go."

We got there early, paid our $10 each, and went into the small auditorium, soon to be joined by 150 other folks who were old enough to remember when Linda was a music icon. The band was put together by her brother, Michael, and included two of his sons. The music was an eclectic mix of Southwestern and Mexican songs, with touches of folk, blues, and jazz.

The room was small enough, the band was close enough, the folks were friendly enough, that it felt like a jam session in your garage. The audience skewed older and greyer but they tapped their feet, clapped their hands, and nodded their heads. At the end, the band did a slow, soulful, and sorrowful rendition of "Ghost Riders in the Sky":

Their faces gaunt, their eyes were blurred,
their shirts all soaked with sweat
He's ridin' hard to catch that herd,
but he ain't caught 'em yet.

It took me back fifty years to Vaughn Monroe and a single 45 RPM I played on my portable record player as a kid. It was a great way to end an afternoon in the desert, and we finished it off with a burger and fries at a cowboy bar and restaurant across the road. We drove back to Green Valley as the sun was setting.

Music is essential to the spiritual journey Cindy and I are trying to share. She's never strayed from the path: going to church, singing in the choir, saying her prayers. I spent thirty-five years as the prodigal son, thinking I held the key and had the answers. I finally figured out that proof was not part of the equation; faith was needed.

I'm beginning to feel it more often now, especially when we attend a Taize prayer service at the Basilica of St. Mary's in downtown Minneapolis. We drive to it in rush hour, sit in the basement on hard wooden chairs, and sing the same verse over and over again.

The light is low, the room is quiet, the candles are lit, and the scene is inviting. It doesn't hurt that we're accompanied by a piano, flute, and sometimes a cello, all beautifully played. We sing together; I try to follow the melody as Cindy sings harmony.

Now I'm not burdened with the usual concerns, causes, and conflicts. If there's a flow, I'm in it. If there's a pattern, I'm part of it.

Calm me Lord as you calmed the storms.
Still me Lord, keep me from harm.
Let all the tumult within me cease.
Enfold me Lord, in your peace.

Cindy and me at Arches National Park

Cindy and I also find that peace together when we're outside walking a trail, a path, or a sidewalk. We've walked on the Pacific Crest Trail in California, the path along the Cascade River on Lake Superior's North Shore, and a ribbon of asphalt around Colby Lake in Woodbury.

Our first real hike was to Eagle Mountain on the North Shore, the highest point in the state. It was a sunny day in July and we clamored over rocks, waded through a bog, glided over moss, and pushed through brush. Along the way we passed a pothole lake with a rocky shoreline and a couple of empty camp sites. When we got to the top, we had the view to ourselves: several lakes in the Boundary Waters Canoe Area below us, sparkling blue against the green of the pine-forest and birch hillsides. I was happy Cindy was at my side, part of an intimate scene and setting.

Almost a decade later, Cindy began having difficulty

walking, caused by an arthritic hip. She started physical therapy as the first step, and the therapist told her to use a cane. Lo and behold, I had a cane, hanging on the end of a bookcase in my den. The gnarled, wooden stick had belonged to my Aunt Orma, who was the reason I came to Minnesota for my first job.

Orma lived life with the hammer down: She dated a string of guys before she married late in life. She was a tailor, and worked in a defense plant during World War II. She could run a fly rod, steer a boat, walk into a bar and have a beer. She lived to be 101 years old and I gave her cane to Cindy. Somehow, I thought Orma would approve.

She would have been delighted I found a woman neither haunted nor intimidated by my past relationships, who graciously supported and understood my need to be with my ex-wife as Kris was dying. Orma would've admired Cindy's determination, her sense of adventure, and her love for and patience with me. And she'd be happy I learned to love someone again.

Cindy has returned the cane; she has a new hip. She's back to walking paths, trails, and roads. I plan to be at her side most of the time—even if I'm the one who needs the cane.

Bookended by a Virus

I was a teenager in the 1950s when I had my first memorable encounter with a virus threat. I had the mumps, measles, and chicken pox but they didn't affect me—and most especially not my parents—like the threat of polio.

My best friend, Bob Lederer, and I, were both "only" children. We both worked part-time jobs after school to earn spending money, and our parents occasionally allowed us to take trips together. This was our first trip to Milwaukee—the "big city"—sixty miles by train south of our hometown. We carried cash in a pocket in our shorts and stayed at the YMCA.

But there was a proviso: we were to call our parents twice a day to let them know where we were, what we were doing and, most important, how we were feeling. They were terrified over the polio threat and gave us a few ultimatums: Stay away from crowds. Get plenty of rest. Eat right, not just hamburgers and French fries. Wash your hands—often.

In three days, we visited the zoo, walked along Milwaukee's Lake Michigan waterfront, and toured television station WTMJ . And we generally did as our parents asked, except for avoiding hamburgers and fries.

It'd be about sixty-five years later when those parental admonitions became marching orders for my sojourn as a senior citizen. I tried to add one more precaution—a face mask—before Cindy Lamont and I took off on a Southwest flight to Tucson and a three-week stay at the little house in Green Valley she and her sister had inherited.

Turns out I was prescient about the value of masks, long before the CDC, Dr. Fauci, and the buyers at CVS, Walgreens, Target and Walmart. At each, I asked, "Do you have face masks?" At each the reply was preceded by a quizzical look or a slight chuckle. No masks, and neither Cindy nor I wore a mask when we got to Green Valley, a retirement community twenty miles south of Tucson, frequently described as Heaven's Waiting Room. The only time we saw a crowd was for the early-bird supper specials, where a quarter of those birds carried oxygen canisters. I'm glad I don't smoke anymore.

When we got back to the Twin Cities, COVID-19 was more than a vague threat. Within days bars and barber shops, retailers and restaurants, tailor shops and travel agencies, closed down. Citizens were supposed to hole up. And senior communities, especially those with assisted living and memory care, were locking down.

That caused a couple of restless nights since I was about to move into Echo Ridge, a seniors' apartment complex for those over fifty-five. My first fear was that I was moving into a Petri dish of old farts, one of them me. My second was that I might not be able to get into the building. Strangers were forbidden, but since I'd already paid a month's rent, I was classified a resident.

My moving company could come once with the furniture. The books, clothes, dishes, electronics, and foliage would be moved by me: one pot at a time, two boxes at a time, three drawers at a time. I stayed out of the elevator, with its enclosed space, and lugged everything up three flights of stairs—fifty-two of them (I counted).

For the first few weeks, I didn't wear a mask. When I did, I believe I became obsequiously friendly with my fellow residents; after all, I was invading their space during a pandemic so I smiled at all of them behind my mask. I offered a cheery Hello. I even told a woman smoking a cigarette in the parking lot that I liked the smell. She said that was a first.

By the time the movers brought my bed, couch, chairs, and recliner, I had already dismantled my computer, printer, and surround–sound television console with its six speakers, two amplifiers, and one cable receiver. I counted twenty-one separate wires, cords, and connections. The Geek Squad I was counting on was no longer making house calls. I was now my own technician, and I slept fitfully the night before I took wires in hand.

I began at 8:30 a.m. with the computer, printer, and Xfinity tower. I worked slowly, breathed deeply, and moved carefully. Within an hour I was hooked up; it took another three hours to connect the TV. I had to snake speaker wires around chairs and behind tables. I had to connect the output to the input for six speakers: left to left, right to right, front to front.

That done, I had to call Comcast to set up the service. Just the thought made me sweat. *I'm going to wind up with a guy in Bangladesh and my hearing loss will be even more obvious.* Instead, I got connected to a guy in Houston who gave me his first name. So I traded names and revealed my fears. What he was about to tell me, I'd never, ever heard before from a tech guy.

"Grab a chair," he said, "and sit back and I'll have this done for you in five minutes." Those were exactly his words. He spoke to me as a father would to a five-year-old standing at the edge of a swimming pool. When a picture came up on the screen I hollered, "You did it. You did it." I e-mailed his supervisor.

Then I sat down in front of that big-screen, surround-sound television staring at the picture and listening to the voices. You'd have thought I had launched a satellite. The euphoria disappeared in the next week, with bouts of depression and despair. The virus was running wild. George Floyd died on the street under the knee of a Minneapolis cop. Protests gave way to looting and burning and many of the victims were neighbors and small shopkeepers.

The Minneapolis City Council talked of "defunding" the police, though no one seemed to be able to explain what that meant. The President of the United States was talking about withholding money from the U.S. Postal Service, admitting that one of the motives was to suppress voting by mail. This wasn't the kind of country or city I dreamed of living in; my friends were calling from Portland and Los Angeles wondering whether I was safe.

All of it was beyond my control, but my daily routine was not. I enlarged my morning prayer list, moving me a little farther from the center of the universe. I called people I hadn't spoken to in months. I e-mailed a couple of old friends I hadn't connected with in years. I went shopping regularly, hitting Target at 8:30 a.m. and Lunds and Byerlys at noon. I wore a mask, moved quickly, stayed away from crowded aisles and harm's way.

I made more dinners for Cindy and amazed myself with the versatility of the George Foreman Grill. I tried to walk at least two miles every day. It's hard to be despairing when your striding along a woodland path early in the morning, alone and alive, looking and listening. My new favorite place became the Lake Elmo Park Reserve District.

I also renewed gatherings with old friends. We met face-to-face but socially distant at a city park in Afton, a patio at the University of St. Thomas, and a picnic table in front of the Minneapolis Park Board office along the Mississippi River. The coffee came from a drive-through and the lunch was take-out, but it beat the devil out of a ZOOM session.

Best of all was the time I spent fishing in my boat. The rest of the world was parked on shore and I was at peace on the water. I fished with old friends, young kids, and expert anglers. During the height of the virus. I went crappie fishing with one of those old friends. We caught our limit of crappies, and after I docked the boat, I tried to sling the stringer up on the dock. I fell over backwards and bounced off the sharp edge of the trolling battery.

I felt a stab of pain and then noticed a trickle of blood running down my side into the waistband of my jeans. Once I got to my feet I coughed a couple of times. No blood in the saliva, so I concluded I hadn't punctured a lung. I finished the trip gamely, eating a sandwich with my friend in the Afton City Park. I assured him I was just fine.

That assurance faded as I drove home. It hurt to take a deep breath, and I began to think I might have broken or fractured a couple of ribs. I stopped at one of those "Urgency" clinics on Valley Creek Road in Woodbury. A nurse wearing a mask and a plastic face cover came up to the car window. She said the clinic was only seeing those who suspected they had the virus.

It was my ribs, I explained, that needed attention. I told her what happened. She said there was another clinic about eight miles away where I could get an X-ray. But then she smiled and said, "I'd suggest time and patience." I decided that beat the hell out of driving eight miles, so I went home, took some ibuprofen, and slept poorly for three nights. After a week, I was good as new.

Time and patience. Maybe I ought to try that again sometime.

About the Author

Dave Nimmer was born and raised in Fond du Lac, Wisconsin, graduated from the University of Wisconsin, and moved to Minnesota in 1963. He worked as a reporter and managing editor for the *Minneapolis Star*, became a reporter and assistant news director at WCCO Television, and taught journalism at the University of St. Thomas for 11 years.

Now retired, Nimmer lives in Oakdale, Minnesota. He is active as a volunteer with the Visitation Monastery of North Minneapolis and the North4 program of Emerge, a non-profit involved in workforce training and community development in Minneapolis. In his spare time, Nimmer likes to hike, fish, and do yard work for his friend and partner at her home in Hudson, Wisconsin. Among the items he carries around are an AARP card, a fishing license, and a lifetime pass to America's national parks.